Alive With Color

Discover
The Secrets of
The Color Clock

The Colors of Morning

THE SUNRISE PALETTE

Alive With Color

The Total Color System
For Women & Men

Leatrice Eiseman

The Sunrise (A.M.) **colortime palette** includes the dewy colors most often associated with early daylight. After a brief splash of brilliant dawn, morning sparkles forth optimistically. Many A.M. colors are pure, clean, transparent, or frosty, with cool blue undertones.

If these colors attract and appeal to you, Alive with Color will show you how to dress, decorate, even energize yourself with the Sunrise colortime palette.

ACROPOLIS BOOKS LTD.
Washington, D.C.

Photo: H. Armstrong Roberts

ACROPOLIS BOOKS, LTD.
Colortone Building, 2400 17th St., N.W.,
Washington, D.C. 20009

Printed in the United States of America by
COLORTONE PRESS
Creative Graphics, Inc.
Washington, D.C. 20009

Attention: Schools and Corporations
ACROPOLIS books are available at quantity discounts with
bulk purchase for educational, business, or sales promotional
use. For information, please write to: SPECIAL SALES
DEPARTMENT, ACROPOLIS BOOKS LTD., 2400 17th
ST., N.W., WASHINGTON, D.C. 20009.

**Are there Acropolis Books you want but cannot find in your
local stores?**
You can get any Acropolis book title in print. Simply send
title and retail price, plus 50 cents per copy to cover mailing
and handling costs for each book desired. District of Colum-
bia residents add applicable sales tax. Enclose check or
money order only, no cash please, to: ACROPOLIS BOOKS
LTD., 2400 17th ST., N.W., WASHINGTON, D.C. 20009.

Library of Congress Cataloging in Publication Data

Eiseman, Leatrice.

    Alive with color.

    Includes index.

    1. Color—Psychological aspects. I. Title.
BF789.C7E37 1983   155.9′1145   83-2838
ISBN 0-87491-552-X

Dedication

To Herb, my dear husband, for his help and encouragement; and to Bea and Ben and to Lori for her beautiful photographs. To Ken and Aunt Lilyan, and the rest of my family and friends for being so supportive and such good listeners.

To Al, Muriel and John Hackl for loving color as much as I do. To Robert Hickey, my wonderfully creative Art Director, and his able associate, Chris Jones. To Kathleen Hughes, whose intelligence, grace and homemade pea soup have nurtured me. To Laurie Tag and Sandy Trupp for their good humor, friendship and hard work; my editors Valerie and Phyllis Avedon, and all of the other special people at Acropolis who make this book happen. To Dene Hofheinz-Anton, Shirley Webb, Christine Torres, and Stan Taylor for their special efforts; and to my fellow members of the Color Marketing Group for their assistance. To Kay Sarazin, Jeff Angell, Frank Westmore, and Vicki Sanchez for sharing their expertise. And to all of the marvelous clients and celebrities who gave me the gift of their time.

Contents

Part I What Color Can Do for You

The Sunrise Palette . . . The Sunset Palette . . . The
Sunlight Palette . . . Color Your Thinking . . .
Creating Your "Ambiance" . . . Exploding Old Myths
. . . White Doesn't Go with Everything!

What To Do if Your Chair (or Hair) Is Fading . . .
For Women Only . . . For Men Only . . . What Goes
with What . . . Goof-Proof Combinations

Decorating in Your Palette . . . Increasing Color
Confidence . . . Patterned for Success . . . Eliminating
Expensive Mistakes . . . Climbing the Wrong-Colored
Walls . . . Importance of Lighting

Yang or Yin? . . . Colors for Job Interviews . . .
Communicating with Color . . . Power Colors . . .
Confessions of a Closet Organizer . . . Themes and
Schemes

Sunrise (A.M.) Color Samples

To see the full range of Sunrise colors, turn to plate E.

Sunlight (Midday) Color Samples

To see the full range of Sunlight colors, turn to plate M.

Sunset (P.M.) Color Samples

To see the full range of Sunset colors turn to Plate I.

The Colortime Quiz

Which Colortime Are You? Are you Sunrise, Sunlight, or Sunset?

I call this system the "Color Clock," because everything in nature, including color, works on a time clock. We associate certain shadings, tints, values, and intensities with specific times of day.

Answer the following questions without stopping to analyze your responses. Your answers should reflect your immediate reaction to color.

Question 1.

Look at the three palettes on the opposite page. Which one do you like most? Don't choose it on the basis of one particular color, or the colors that you think are most popular now.

Choose the one you really like best. Get a sense of the whole picture and how the colors look together.

Circle one:

        Sunrise   Sunlight   Sunset

Question 2.

If you could completely redecorate your home, which palette has most of the colors you would choose?

Circle one:

        Sunrise   Sunlight   Sunset

Question 3.

If you could buy an entirely new wardrobe, which palette has most of the colors you would choose to wear?

Circle one:

        Sunrise   Sunlight   Sunset

The Colors of Evening

THE SUNSET PALETTE

Question 4.

Look at yourself in a mirror, near natural light if possible. Then answer the following questions to determine your personal coloring. Make the best selections you can from the choices given. Or ask a friend to help you. Mark your answers and tally the results.

What color are your eyes?

Blue

Blue, clear light blue or medium blue ....
Sapphire blue .... Sunrise
Blue, but almost grey ....

Blue with a little grey ....
Peacock blue .... Sunset

Blue, but I don't see myself distinctly in either
   of the above categories .... Sunlight

Brown

Dark, rosy cocoa brown—light medium or dark ....
Very dark brown, almost jet black............................... Sunrise

Amber ....
Warm golden brown—light, medium or dark .... Sunset
Very dark brown ....

Brown, but I don't see myself distinctly in
   any one of the above categories .... Sunlight

Hazel

Grey hazel, a combination of blue, grey,
   and perhaps some green.. Sunrise

(continued)

The Sunset (P.M.) colortime palette includes the colors of the descending sun. As day draws to a close, the fiery sunset radiates with the beautiful, warm P.M. shadings that gradually dissolve into a restful, mellowed dusk.

If these colors attract and appeal to you, Alive with Color *will show you how to dress, decorate, and even relax with the Sunset colortime palette.* Photo: Lori Eiseman

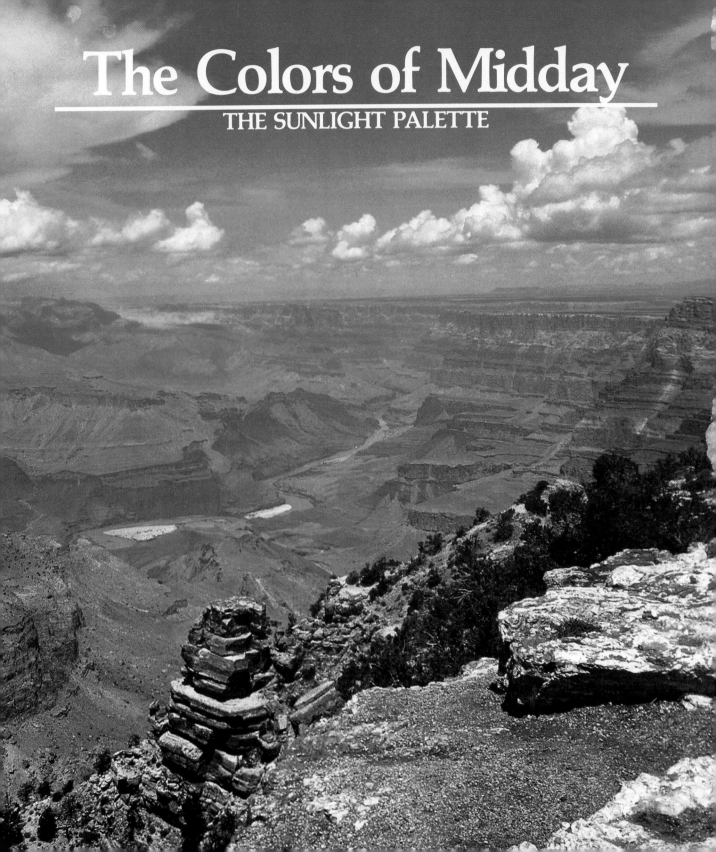

The Colors of Midday

THE SUNLIGHT PALETTE

Golden hazel, a combination of brown, gold,
    green and perhaps some blue .... Sunset

Hazel, I don't see myself distinctly in either of the
    above categories because I have many colors in my eyes .... Sunlight

Green

Bright blue-green ....
Bright green with some yellow undertones .... Sunrise

Greyed blue-green ....
Green gold .... Sunset
Green grey ....

Light or medium blue-green, but I don't see myself as
    being distinctly in any of the above categories..................... Sunlight

What is your hair color?

(If you color your hair, answer this question by giving your youthful
natural hair color.)

Blonde

Ash blonde—light, medium or dark ....
Platinum blonde .... Sunrise
Towhead..

Golden or coppery blonde—light, medium or dark .... Sunset

Blonde—light, medium or dark—but I don't see
    myself as being any of the above. I think I have
    a mixture of the blondes, both warm and cool
    tones together... Sunlight

Red

Auburn, with cool blue undertones............................. Sunrise

Strawberry red ....

(continued)

The Sunlight (Midday) colortime palette reflects the
way the strong sun of noon mutes colors to a subtle
softness. The majestic Grand Canyon at midday vibrates
with the beauty of the Sunlight palette.

   If you feel drawn to these colors, Alive with Color
will show you how to paint your world with interesting,
understated elegance.   *Photo: Herb Eiseman*

Alive
With Color

Golden copper red—light, medium or dark . . . .   Sunset
Rust-wine red, like bordeaux . . . .

Red, but I think I have a combination of
   both warm and cool tones . . . .   Sunlight

Brown

Ash brown—light, medium or dark, but without gold . . . .   Sunrise
Dark brown, may have auburn highlights . . . .

Golden brown—light, medium or dark—
   sometimes with copper highlights . . . .   Sunset

Brown—light, medium or dark—but I don't see myself
   clearly in any of the above categories. I have both
   warm and cool tones mixed together . . . .   Sunlight

Black

Blue-black . . . .   Sunrise

Brown-black . . . .   Sunset

Grey

Snow white . . . .   Sunrise
Silver grey, with cool blue undertones . . . .

Cream white . . . .
Winter white . . . .   Sunset
Pewter grey (not as blue grey as silver) . . . .

Grey, but I don't see myself as being distinctly
   in any of the above categories. I'm a mixture . . . .   Sunlight

What is your skin tone?

(Often people are unsure of their precise skin tone. If you have difficulty answering this question, don't worry. Just pick the answer that
you think comes closest to describing your coloring.)

Olive

Olive with green undertones . . . .   Sunrise

Olive with warm golden undertones . . . .   Sunset

Olive, light, but I don't think I belong
in either of the above categories .... Sunlight

Black or Brown

Blue-black.. Sunrise
Rosey brown ....

Golden honey brown (light, medium, or dark)..................... Sunset

Very light brown .... Sunlight

Fair

Fair, cool white .... Sunrise

Warm, creamy white .... Sunset

Ivory .... Sunlight

Beige

Rose beige .... Sunrise
Rose pink ....

Warm peach beige (light, medium, or deep) .... Sunset

Beige, but I have a mixture of both rose
and peach tones .... Sunlight

Score your answers to Question 4

My eye color is	☐ Sunrise	☐ Sunset	☐ Sunlight
My hair color is	☐ Sunrise	☐ Sunset	☐ Sunlight
My skin tone is	☐ Sunrise	☐ Sunset	☐ Sunlight

If you marked two or three in one column, this is definitely yours. If you marked one in each colortime, go with Sunlight. Sunlight is a balanced combination of both Sunrise and Sunset, so it's a no-fail compromise. You may decide later that you have an emotional attachment to one palette or another, and change your mind. But more about this later. Stick to Sunlight for now.

Now, turn to page 18, and read the section entitled QUIZ EXPLANATION.

I am a confessed color addict! Even as a small child, my hair ribbons and socks always had to match my dress. Coloring books were my favorite pastime and my crayons were worn to stumps. Color combinations reflected my mood of the moment, especially the bizarre (but I thought very sophisticated) glossy black and tomato red combination I chose for my room when I was 16!

In looking back, I realize that my mother's passion for the paintbrush must have been a major influence in my life. Almost every year, she would go through the house painting everything in sight that didn't move, including the piano.

I don't know how the people who bought that piano years later moved it out of the house. It must have weighed a ton with those 25-odd (some of them *very* odd) coats of paint!

One year she outdid herself by painting an old metal toaster a not terribly attractive chartreuse. Someone mistakenly used it and the house reeked of smoke for weeks. My mother retired from painting for a while after that, so we lived with chartreuse for a long time. It remains one of my un-favorite colors to this day.

In college, art and psychology were two of my favorite subjects. I devoured information on color. I read, studied, and researched every color-related topic I could get my hands on. In the early years of my career as director of education for a group of self-improvement schools, when I researched curriculum and trained the teachers, color was invariably the subject that claimed most of my attention.

Presently, as an Image and Color Consultant, I lecture and hold seminars for colleges, professional organizations, industrial groups, and conventions, and consult with individual clients and entertainers. My audiences are diverse; they include interior designers, hospital administrators, homemakers, hobbyists, makeup artists, hair colorists, dentists, doctors, florists, costume and set designers, wardrobe consultants—people interested in color, which includes just about everyone! Although they come from all walks of life, they have one thing in common—they're fascinated with color and want to know more about it.

My clients have taught me, in the process of exploring their natural color preferences, as much as I have taught them. One of the most important things I have learned about color is that you never stop learning about it, because color "rules" are never so rigid that they cannot be adapted to individual needs.

Those of you with a well-developed sense of color will find that this book helps you understand why you make your color choices. If you are a professional who deals with color, it may open new avenues of thinking—it can certainly help you deal more objectively with your clients.

Those of you who are simply interested in the subject will not only find out about the "how-to's," but about the "why-do-I's" of color choices.

The purpose of this book is to share my discoveries with you so that you may enrich your life, as I have mine, and learn to be alive with color!

The system I use is called your "Color Clock." It can literally change your life and can certainly simplify it. Among the things you will learn are:

1. How to use color to make you feel more secure, successful, tranquil, stimulated, or happy.

2. What color to paint your house if you want to sell it.

3. Which colors to avoid if you need to lose weight.

4. Why to be wary if your mate loves orange.

5. How to raise the roof or shrink a sofa.

6. Which colors raise your energy level.

7. How to avoid expensive mistakes with color.

8. How to use color—with confidence—to bring out your creativity.

9. What goes with what and why.

10. Most importantly, the Color Clock will help you to discover how to feel in harmony with the world around you—your total environment—through your personal colortime palette.

Before you learn about your own personal colortime, it is important to take the *Color Quiz* on page 9 to establish your preferences. Please be sure to take the quiz before you read the explanation.

Quiz Explanation

After analyzing the preferences of thousands of students, clients, and audiences, I know that the colortime that people choose in question 1 is likely to be the one they also choose in questions 3 and 4. Most people will discover that the colortime palette that contains their skin, hair, and eye color is their preferred palette. They will often, but not always, choose that same colortime palette for their surroundings. Your natural color sense draws you to those colors.

You are part of nature's Grand Design. A misused hair tint can cause a hair color mistake, but you can't fool Mother Nature. You are born with blending skin, hair, and eye color. Everything in nature is designed to blend.

Study the color of Siamese cats and you will see how their eyes, fur, noses, and foot pads all blend into a particular colortime. Look at Irish setter puppies in a pet store window—all of their golden colors fit into the Sunset palette.

Go back to question 4 to make certain that you chose the best colors. Check your eye color first in a good light. You may discover colors in your eyes you've never seen before. Brown-eyed people are often amazed when I point out the green in their eyes. Take the time to really study yourself. Look at the undertones in your skin and hair. That's a really interesting person staring back at you in the mirror, and he or she deserves this attention.

If you find it hard to be objective, ask a friend to help you. It's often easier when someone else helps you judge your coloring. If two out of the three personal colorings, such as your eyes and hair, are in one of the palettes, you can feel assured that it is your palette. If you color your hair, try to find your natural hair color on the list. Many times clients tell me that they can't remember—it's been so long since they've seen it! Ask an old friend or your hairdresser, if he or she is the only one who knows "for sure."

Look at the clothes in your closet. Since you do most of the choosing (assuming that someone else has not done the choosing for you), most of the colors will be in your colortime. The colors in your home are a less accurate indication of your colortime because other people are often involved in your choices, or because you had to work with colors that

Alive
With Color

19

were already there when you moved in, such as carpeting or tile. But if you did the decorating and are really happy with your choices, the colors that you chose can also help you find your colortime.

If, however, you are not happy with your choices in either your clothing or your home, or you're just ready for a change, the following discussion can help you determine which colortime to use. This may be just the time for your personal Declaration of Independence!

Where Your Choices Take You — More About You

If you circled the same colortime palette in answer to all four questions, you should have little trouble choosing colors because you have a really strong affinity for the particular colortime palette that you circled—Sunrise, Sunlight, or Sunset. You will feel your absolute best when you wear and are surrounded by the colors in that color-time. That's the good news.

The bad news is that because you have this strong pull in one direction, you might be somewhat inflexible in decisions involving someone in another colortime (husband, wife, business partner, teen-aged daughter, others involved in planning a wedding, etc.).

You are not, however, apt to be confused about your colortime. People are likely to ask for your advice because you are so decisive—but you're likely to advise them to use *your* favorite colors!

We are most likely to choose our clothing colors from the same palette that contains our skin, hair, and eye colors. But if the palette you circled for question 2, about the colors you would choose for your home is different from the other palettes, you could be content to "dress" your surroundings in a different colortime than the one in which you dress yourself.

Your clothing should reflect your personal coloring, but your home may reflect a particular mood from another colortime. We'll get into those moods later. You are more flexible than the person mentioned earlier who has chosen the same palette throughout, but the bad news here is that you may have difficulty making a decision because you are so flexible.

Is it possible to favor two colortime palettes equally? The answer to that question is "Yes." You could probably be happy using any of the colortime palettes you circled. In terms of decorating, your choices give you more freedom to convey different moods. You might choose to do a bedroom in the Sunlight palette, and the kitchen in the Sunset palette, for example, and perhaps a child's room in the Sunrise palette.

You are probably delightful to work with because of your flexibility, but may find it hard to decide which palette to use and where. Extra freedom of choice can mean extra confusion!

I often advise clients to go with their hearts and not with their heads. The color that gives you that emotional tug is the one you want to use. If you analyze and agonize too much, you lose the point of what color is all about.

With clothing choices, I feel it's best to choose the colortime palette that contains your personal skin, hair, and eye coloring and stay with it most of the time—it's more flattering and makes you look your best. It is also more practical, easier on the budget, and everything you wear will blend well with other colors in the same colortime. If, however, you have a really favorite color in another colortime, there are ways to integrate that color into your wardrobe. We'll get into that later.

If you have a strong aversion to a particular colortime, then you obviously should avoid using it because it will make you uncomfortable to be surrounded by that palette. You are also likely to be definite about your other dislikes. This shouldn't become a problem unless you're living with or sharing an office with someone who absolutely loves that colortime. There are compromises, which we will also explore later.

Have you ever gotten a sweater from someone in a color that you felt looked awful on you? Chances are that it was in the giver's color-time—not yours. They may have spent hours knitting it and think it's just wonderful. You can begin to solve that problem by telling everyone what your colortime colors are—they may take the hint the next time they give you something.

Should you experiment with a colortime that you didn't circle? Chances are that you won't want to, but trends do tempt you, your lifestyle may change, and your moods definitely do, so that you feel the need to try something totally different. And unless you live alone, you also have other people to consider.

My experience has been that you will tire more quickly of colors that are not included in your preferred colortime as indicated by the quiz. It's risky to experiment in a large area when you're investing a lot of money.

Try these colors instead in a basement recreation room, a small powder room, or on your patio—some fun place where you can change colors inexpensively with a coat or two of paint, should you decide later that those trendy colors aren't really you at all.

Try a different colortime in an inexpensive piece of clothing or accessory before you invest a whole paycheck on something that may turn out to be a mistake.

Did you circle all of the colortimes for all of the answers? You are the kind of person who says "I love all colors!" That sounds wonderful and you're very flexible—but somewhat fickle and definitely moody!

Just like a kid in a candy store, you may want "two of those," and "three of these," and, wait a minute—another "one of those." Some of my wildest (but most fun) clients say they like *everything*. And they *want* everything . . . sometimes all in the same room or in the same outfit.

If this sounds like you, there are three ways for you to avoid becoming totally uncoordinated.

1. In clothing, go with the palette that contains your personal coloring, for the most flattering and organized solution. If you still feel that you want to wear all three palettes, don't combine them all in one outfit. It does mean that you will have three separate wardrobe palettes, each of which needs blending accessories and, if you're a woman, blending makeup colors.

2. In a home, use all colortimes, but use each in a different area. The result may be a house of many moods, but you probably have the personality to handle it!

3. Use the Sunlight colortime palette because it overlaps into both the Sunrise and Sunset palettes and offers you a wide, but more subtle, range of choices.

If you're having difficulty finding your own coloring in one particular palette, or you simply cannot decide which pleases you the most, then I suggest that you also go with the Sunlight colortime. This palette is a happy compromise and because your own coloring is likely to be so varied that it is difficult for you to see which palette is yours, you may belong right in the middle with the Sunlight palette.

Do colortime choices ever change? In some people they do, in others, they stay constant over a lifetime. Your coloring may change as you age. Your hair may start to grey and soften your look. Your skin may (but not always) start to pick up more yellow with age. (Think of handsome lace or cotton—not old newspapers!)

Your eyes do fade, but that can be an advantage because the

undertones then begin to come through and you can introduce these colorings into your wardrobe.

You may have been born a Sunrise and loved many of this palette's bright shades as a child and young adult. But as nature ages and softens your coloring, you might want to switch to the softer Sunlight palette. Then again, your coloring may remain fairly constant, especially if you color your hair, and you may continue to wear the same colors you wore when you were younger.

Elizabeth Taylor will always look wonderful in Sunrise colors. The vivid contrasts of her dark hair, light skin, and violet eyes will continue to allow her to wear accents of brilliant colors, or the stark contrast of black and white. **Cary Grant's** hair went from darkest dark to whitest white, but the same blue-wine ties are as elegant on him today as they were in his old movies. **Lucille Ball** is an eternal Sunset. Can you imagine that inimitable redhead ever going grey?

Ed Asner's colortime quiz indicates a strong preference for the Sunset colortime. He favors oranges, rusts, and earth tones, but also likes the lighter variations of these colors. He was born with Sunset coloring — warm skin, hair, and eye color. But his hair (and sometimes his beard—depending on the role) are now a mixture of greys and brown and his eyes have lightened.

He should stay with the Sunset colors for his environment, because they please him so much, but the Sunlight colors, especially the warmer and neutral combinations, will look best on him now that his coloring is variegated.

Don't let the existence of many different types of coloring in each colortime confuse you. There are light, medium, and dark colorings in each palette. All you need to do is to look at the closest description of hair, skin, and eyes in each colortime list to come up with the right combination for you.

"Dynasty's" **Linda Evans** has cool, ash blonde hair, rose-beige skin, and grey-blue eyes. **Lynda "Wonder Woman" Carter** has blue-black hair, fair-rose skin, and clear light blue eyes. Both women are combinations of the Sunrise palette and wear many of the same colors beautifully. My clients are often amazed to see how individuals with coloring that appears to be so different on the surface can actually wear many of the same colors.

Within racial or ethnic groups, there are many variations. All "black" skins are obviously not black, and racial or ethnic groups should be studied carefully for undertones. **Bryant Gumbel** of the "Today" show is a Sunset with his light golden brown skin, honey brown eyes and deeper brown hair. **Flip Wilson** has darker brown skin with a rose undertone, deep rose-brown eyes, and even darker hair. He is a Sunrise.

Oriental skins may fall into any of the three colortimes. Some orientals have very blue-black hair and eyes, with the cool green olive undertones of Sunrise; others have the deep but very warm hair and eye coloring and warm olive skin of Sunset. If you are of mixed racial background, you may fall into the Sunlight palette.

Ruddy or florid skins may also be found in all three palettes, so basing your choice on hair and eye color may be the best way to find out which palette is yours. For example, a florid skin may typically be found in redheads, or redheads who have gone grey. If their eyes and hair have warm undertones, even though the skin is flushed, they will be in the Sunset palette.

Let your initial, emotional, reaction to the three palettes be your guide, if you are in doubt, and you will find yourself in your best colortime.

Choices—"Right" or "Wrong"

It is important to remember that there are no "right" or "wrong" answers to any quiz in this book. No one is going to give you a poor grade and make you stand in a colorless corner if you make the "wrong" choices.

You cannot make a mistake in choosing your colortime palette, because colortime choices are simply a question of personal, natural reactions. I am not placing you in a little color cubicle and asking you not to stray from it.

I would never presume to tell you what your colortime is without first asking you how you feel about certain colors. Since I can't be right there with you, the quiz stands in for me by asking the questions that I would ask.

When I do seminars, classes, or conventions, I take three large collages with me, one in each colortime. I ask for volunteers to stand in front of the chart they relate to best. It is interesting to me that children have no problem at all in doing this; they are so "free" and uninhibited. But adults become very analytical and self-conscious and often choose colors because of what a friend in the audience suggests. Your friend—wonderful person that he or she may be—cannot tell you how you feel or what you see.

A man in a recent convention audience stood up in front of a collage that he was obviously uncomfortable with. His body language was the giveaway—he kept edging away from the collage and would never really look directly at it. When I asked him why he would choose a colortime that he really didn't like, he said that those were the colors that his wife always decorated the house (and him) with. I asked him to bring her up from the audience, but he told me that would be a little difficult—she had been dead for ten years!

That poor, dear man was hanging on to the same old colors because his wife had been a very strong lady and he had allowed her to do his choosing for him. He just didn't know how to make his own choices and stayed with the old familiar ones out of habit. Are you doing the same?

You may have been surprised by your response to the quiz. Did you find yourself in a palette you would never have expected to be in? That should tell you something. Maybe it's time for a change—go for it!

The man whose color environment was based on his departed wife's choices became a client of mine. He redid his house, his clothes, his office, his life, joined a singles' group, and remarried!

Part I

What Color
Can Do
For You

Chapter 1

Discover the Secrets of The Color Clock

What is the Color Clock?

I call this system the "Color Clock," because everything in nature, including color, works on a time clock. We associate certain shadings, tints, values, and intensities with specific times of day.

Writers and poets traditionally use colors to describe various hours. Dawn is apt to be "cold and grey." Sunshine is invariably yellow. And cowboys always ride off into a "blazing golden sunset"!

Inspiration of the Impressionists

The Impressionist painters transformed art history with their efforts to capture the full impression of nature and the play of light on a particular scene at a particular time. Impressionist **Claude Monet,** renowned for his magical studies of water lilies, often painted the same subject to show how its colors varied at different times of the day.

Colors do appear to vary during the course of a day because of changing light and the presence of various particles that float around in the atmosphere.

Look at the illustrations of the colortimes. You will note that Sunrise is also called "AM," Sunset, "PM," and Sunlight, "Midday."

The Colortime Palettes

In the earliest hours of the day, warm color begins to emerge from the cold, grey dawn. A rosy glow appears before the dazzling sun actually begins its ascent. Because sunrise is sunset in reverse, the shadings progress from the darkness of blue and grey to purpled rose-mauves to the splendor of the red-orange glow. But because the atmosphere is generally cleaner and more moist in the morning, the colors of sunrise are much less fiery than those of sunset. This dewy "wetness" permeates the Sunrise colortime.

Occasionally, when the air is very clean, there is a clear green streak across the sky just after the dawn breaks. Later in the morning, the sun changes into a brilliant yellow-white. Blues are brightest in the early hours and the sky is at its clearest.

An undertone of cool blue pervades most of the Sunrise (AM) colortime.

In the afternoon, you see the Sunset (PM) colors. As the number of yellowed dust particles in the atmosphere increases at this time of day, most colors appear to take on a golden, hazy, or mellow quality. Colors appear "drier" than they do in the morning.

In the late afternoon, as the sun goes down, you see the fiery shades of sunset. Gold is the pervading undertone of sunset's orange, rust, warm reds, and curried greens. At dusk, the spectral rays of deep blue take over, often combining with the reflected reds to become a red-violet glow.

In the very middle of the clock, between 10 a.m. and 2 p.m., is the Sunlight (Midday) colortime palette. The intensity of the sun is greatest during these hours. Even when the sun is covered by clouds, the force of its reflected light remains strong. Any object that receives direct sunlight during these hours seems slightly diminished, because intense light dazzles the eye and makes the colors appear somewhat muted.

Since this colortime is derived from both the AM and PM palettes, it offers the widest range of choices, but the colors are subtle—they never scream. This is the palette of pleasing, luscious pastels of every hue. Any of the tints may be deepened to a darker value for contrast.

Charcoal, black, and navy blue represent the shades of night and pre-dawn when all colors are shrouded in darkness. They may be used with all of the colortime palettes. They are part of "Nature's Crossover Colors" and are explained more fully later in this chapter. The crossover colors are part of every palette.

As the sun travels around the clock, you see that every color in the spectrum is represented throughout the daytime hours. Mother Nature does not exclude any color from any segment of the clock. She simply varies the undertones, intensities, and values in each colortime palette.

Let's go to the Colortime Quiz to find out about your natural harmonies. The quiz helped you identify your colortime preference. Now you'll find the colors that belong in each colortime.

Which Colortime Are You...
SUNRISE...   SUNLIGHT...   SUNSET?

The Sunrise (AM) Colortime Palette

If you chose the Sunrise palette for your clothing and/or interiors, the natural elements of water and air are a strong influence on the predominantly cool blue undertones of your colortime palette. The illustration on Plate E shows samples of those colors.

Your palette literally sparkles, and many of your colors are such "jewel" and "royal" tones as:

Amethyst	Sapphire Blue
Opalescent Teal	Ruby Red
Regal Purple	Emerald Green
Bright Turquoise	Windsor Blue
Aquamarine	Fuchsia

The cool colors are often transparent and frosty:

Ice Blue	Crystal Grey
Snow White	Lavender Frost
Aqua	Celestial Blue
Seafoam Green	Orchid Dawn
Mauve Morn	

The warm colors in your palette are pure and cooled down:

Shell Pink	Watermelon
Rose-Pink Coral	Sea Pink
Raspberry Glace	Misted Rose
Cherry Red	Shocking Pink

The kelly and lime greens of your palette are fresh, clean, and bright, as are daffodil and daybreak yellows.

Orange and red-orange play a very small role in your colortime and are usually least favored by people choosing this palette. Use them sparingly as accents, just as nature does in the short time span of sunrise. Oranges will work best for you when you lighten them to rosy pink-corals or deepen them to rich cocoa and bittersweet browns.

Grey, rose-beige, and mauve-taupe are natural neutrals for your palette.

Your best white is pure white.

Famous people who share your Sunrise colortime are:

Elizabeth Taylor	Paul Newman	Princess Diana
Lynda Carter	Flip Wilson	Linda Evans
Cristina DeLorean	Liza Minnelli	Erik Estrada
Cary Grant	Christopher Reeve	Stephanie Mills

The Sunset (PM) Colortime Palette

Did you circle the Sunset Colortime for your clothing and/or room settings? If you did, you prefer the Sunset (PM) Colortime palette. The natural elements of fire and earth are a strong influence on the predominantly golden undertones of your colortime.

Your palette is primarily warm and is often described as "earthy." The warm, spicy shades are important to you.

Cinnamon   Paprika

But you should not be so "down-to-earth" that you do not enjoy a touch of the exotic:

Curry   Avocado

These greens can give special flavor to your life:

Bay Leaf   Dill

Your taste can also be tempted with the sweet shades of:

Honey   Apricot
Peach

Other earth colors that are important to this colortime are:

Brick Red	Terra Cotta
Bronze	Camel
Bordeaux	Harvest Gold

Your light to medium pinks are best when they are dusty and warm, like ash rose and coral dust.

In addition to the spice greens, hunter, warm taupe, and khaki are basic to your colortime. The fiery portion of the Sunset palette is reflected in tomato red, red-purple, burnt orange, geranium, and hazy magenta.

Your cool colors are the mellowed:

Heathered Purple	Deep Teal
Lilac Dusk	Peacock
Dusk Blue	Antique Turquoise
Cadet Blue	Smoke Grey
Deep Periwinkle	

The colors you should use most sparingly are strong shocking pinks. Mother Nature uses these hues in brief splashes, and so should you.

Your best white is cream.

Examples of famous "Sunset people" include:

Victoria Principal	Melissa Gilbert
Stephanie Powers	Natalie Cole
Connie Chung	Telly Savalas
Lynn Redgrave	Robert Redford
Ed Asner	Lorenzo Lamas
Bryant Gumbel	Barbra Streisand
Jane Fonda	Rita Moreno

The Sunlight (Midday) Colortime Palette

Did you circle Sunlight for your clothing and/or interiors? If you did, your preference is for the Sunlight (Midday) colortime palette.

This colortime dips into both Sunrise and Sunset. Yours are the softened, muted, sun-drenched tints. They are more intense than pale pastels, never "wishy-washy" or nondescript.

Any of the natural elements of air, water, fire, and earth are present in your palette, but they are never flamboyant. The hot shades of Sunset would overwhelm this palette, but dusty rose is perfect. The sapphire blue of Sunrise would work better if gentled to the muted tones of Limoges.

The tints and shadings are the delicious ice cream, sherbet, and confection colors. This is the fattening palette. A Baskin-Robbins ice cream store would be a perfect place to check out your best colors, but if you are dieting, try a fruit stand instead.

Your warm shades are truly delectable:

Peach Melba	Lemonade
Buttercream	Strawberry Cream
Melon	Raspberry Sherbet
Banana	Bisque
Mocha	Creme Caramel

The colors of the plates on which you serve your food describe some of your best blues:

Wedgwood	Delft
China	Limoges

Your other cool shades are subtle and interesting:

Grape	Creme de Menthe
Plum Cordial	Soft Turquoise
Orchid	Teal

Mauve	Celadon
Jade	Wisteria
Lilac	

Your greens include a sprinkle of Mint and Sage.

Because your colors are gathered from both the AM and PM palettes, you can express yourself especially well with such variegated combinations as neutral tweeds with small flecks of color, subtle checks, or plaids. Avoid really bright colors; they won't work as well for you and are best used as an added touch.

Subtle is a key word for Midday palettes. If given a choice, opt for the subtle. True red is the best of the brights for Midday, but avoid using it in neon intensities. Fiery orange is not a good choice for this palette. Lighten it to orange blossom or deepen it to chestnut, and you will be much happier with it.

Any of your colors may be deepened in value. You may prefer evergreen to creme de menthe, or wine to mauve when the occasion calls for a little more dignity or sophistication.

Neutral taupes such as sand, bark, and mushroom, and dove greys combine well with both the warm and the cool hues of your colortime, and since neutrals are never noisy, they will also work best for you.

Your best white is vanilla—not too pure and not too creamy. "Almost" whites with pastel undertones are also good.

Examples of famous "Sunlight" colortime people include:

Candice Bergen	Kristy McNichol
Cheryl Tiegs	Kris Kristofferson
Olivia Newton-John	Lee Remick
Dr. Rick Weber	Katharine Hepburn
Prince Charles	Jane Curtin

What Color Can Do For You

Color is an essential ingredient in the enhancement of your environment. It can direct and divert the eye, communicate emotion, create moods and optical illusions, delight, or dignify. It has enormous influence in your life, starting from the day you were first able to discern the colors in the world around you.

Nature's paintbox yields wonderful possibilities. There are limitless tints or tones to excite you or calm you, elate you or depress you, warm you or cool you. Color may heighten your awareness and make you more sensitive to your surroundings.

Color can enhance your self-image and make you feel marvelous. I have seen some amazing changes after having helped clients find their personal palettes. One of the first messages you give to other people before you ever say a word is "spoken" in the colors you use. Haven't you walked into someone's home and instantly felt warm and comfortable? You knew you were going to like that person even before you two met. You were responding to the universal silent language of color.

An "Eye" For Color

Is an "eye" for color like an "ear" for music? Are we born with a sense of color? I think both of these questions can be answered "yes" and "no." Some experts feel that we may be predisposed to certain abilities through artistic ancestors, whereas others believe an "eye" for color is acquired through the learning process.

You don't have to be born a child prodigy to play the piano. Through instruction and practice you can learn to play well enough to satisfy your needs. You may never perform like Billy Joel or the late Artur Rubinstein, but you can still get a sense of satisfaction and enjoyment out of playing.

The same holds true for color. You may not have been born with artistic ability, but you can learn how to use color so that it will work wonders for you and give you tremendous satisfaction. When you arrange flowers in a vase, take a photograph, or serve food on a plate, you are the artist.

Affinity and Attraction

Af-fin-i-ty: *The relationship existing between persons or things that are naturally or involuntarily drawn together.*

At-trac-tion: *To draw by appeal to natural or excited interest, emotion, or esthetic sense.*

What You See

You have a natural affinity for or attraction to certain colors and colortimes. When you walk by a flower shop and see many beautiful arrangements, one or two will catch your eye. There may be a big selection to choose from, but some are more special to you than others. Texture, scent, and design will also attract you, but color often draws your attention first.

What you see pleases your esthetic sense—your appreciation of beauty. Some of the bouquets are so special to you that they almost take your breath away. You are attracted to certain colors because they are in tune with your natural colortime preferences.

What You Feel

Decorating magazines are full of handsome rooms, but some beckon to you more than others. Some seem so comfortable to you that you wish you could climb right into the picture. There is an almost irresistible influence that tugs at you and appeals to your emotions. What you feel pleases you.

One of my clients, **Kay S.,** redecorates every few years, invariably in beiges and browns. She felt that she was in a color rut, but explained that those colors just felt so natural to her. When we got into a discussion about that particular combination, we discovered that her school uniform had been beige and brown. Several clients have turned away from the colors that they had to wear for years (such as army fatigue green), but Kay had pleasant memories—she adored her school years, remembering them as the happiest time of her life. She was a good student who felt a sense of accomplishment and was secure and popular. I told her that if browns and beiges made her feel all of those good things, she should continue to use them.

Many people make the mistake of switching to "new" colors simply because of the novelty. They soon grow tired of their selections and realize they never felt quite comfortable in that environment.

If the same colors continue to make you happy over the years, there's no need to switch. Often a touch of an interesting accent color is all that is necessary for a new look. In Kay's case, I suggested touches of teal and tomato from her PM colortime palette to add a little pizazz.

Color Your Thinking

At this point, you may be thinking, "If I have this natural affinity, why is it that I may not be happy with my color choices?" There are several explanations:

1. You allow too many outside influences to color your thinking (pun intended). These can include family, friends, fads, persuasive advertising, and the bargains you find so hard to resist. Bargains may be marvelous for the budget, but the bargain that sits forgotten in the closet is no bargain. Have you ever chosen carpeting and hated it from the moment it was nailed to the floor? Or tried a bathroom wallpaper and felt that you had contracted instant yellow jaundice when you saw it reflected next to your face in the mirror? Chances are that the color you chose (or that someone else chose for you) was not in your personal colortime.

Do you often give people gifts in the colors you like best? They probably do the same to you! With the Color Clock method, you can let everyone know what your colortime is, and learn to choose colors that will please everyone on your gift list. This will save you money by helping you avoid expensive mistakes.

2. Colors are rarely used in isolation. Choosing one color that you really like may be simple for you. But combining that hue with other shades, tints, and intensities can be troublesome. Don't let finding the correct combination deadlock your efforts. If this is the part that confuses you, read on. The "how to's" and how they work follow in the next chapter.

3. The psychological and emotional impacts of color can delight you or devastate you. It is almost impossible to separate the "seeing" of color from the "feeling" because so much of what you see is based on what you feel. Colors evoke emotions—some pleasant, some very unpleasant. You can turn off to a terrific color because of some experience long past.

Do pink roses make you think of the first prom corsage you ever got (or gave), or do they remind you of the time that you ate too much cotton candy at a carnival and got sick on the way home? Your reaction to a particular color will definitely be influenced by your personal experience.

Certain colors and color combinations can put that wondrous tape recorder in your head on "instant rewind." You never really forget anything you have ever learned. You just deposit it in your memory bank for future withdrawals.

Keeping an Open Mind

Even though you may respond favorably to most colors in your colortime, you may not like every single color because of a previous negative experience you associate with that particular shade. Most of the time you can't even remember what the memory is. Consider the following story:

Martha L. came to me for a color consultation because her husband told her he was sick of her decorating with the "same old nondescript neutrals" and wanted some purples in the house. That instantly told me that her husband was highly creative and unusual. Men rarely like purples for decorating, especially in the lighter values, but this one turned out to be an artist and a very interesting person.

She, however, had a really hard time with anything remotely purple—any shade, including, and most particularly, lavender. I asked Martha to try to remember why she might be having such a difficult time. She thought about it for several days and then called me with this story:

As a child, she had a wonderful loving relationship with her grandmother. The little girl would bring sprigs of lavender to her, since it was her grandmother's favorite color. The grandmother had beautiful Sunrise silver hair and wore the color a great deal. She also loved touches of lavender throughout the house in delicate potpourris.

When my client was 8, her beloved grandmother died. Of course, she was buried in a lavender dress and everyone sent various shades of purple flowers to the funeral. Interestingly, some funeral homes did (and still do) decorate in purples, since in some cultures it is considered a mourning color. A purple wreath was often placed on the front door.

We had all the clues we needed to realize why Martha was so turned off by those colors. It had been her first experience with death and she was so traumatized by it that she simply locked the painful event away in her subconscious. The memories of that difficult day faded but her grandmother's favorite color had become associated in Martha's mind with a deep sense of loss.

When my client asked my help in overcoming her purple prejudice, I gave her the same advice I give to anyone who really wants to become open to trying new colors: For every negative experience, find a positive flip side of pleasurable associations. In this particular case, once the client had remembered the unpleasant associations, she could deal with them and turn to the happier aspects.

There is a delightful P.S. to this story. For her daughter's wedding, the mother of the bride chose—you guessed it—a lavender dress. When I called to congratulate her on her daughter's marriage, she thanked me profusely for opening her up to purple. Now when she looks in the bedroom mirror and sees herself surrounded by the lavender accents, she realizes how much like her grandmother she has become (her AM palette is the same), and what marvelous stories she will be able to tell her own grandchildren.

If she hadn't allowed herself to experience the color, those important years with her grandmother might have remained hidden forever. Few of us have such poignant stores to relate, but we all need to keep an open mind to color. You never know when you might unwrap a beautiful box of memories—all in living color.

Nita Schroeder, a multi-talented lady who is an artist, an author, and now a screenwriter, loves white—anything and everything in white, especially gardenias.

When I asked her if she knew why she was so in love with the color, she only had to think for a moment to remember "two of my favorite people: my 97-year-old great grandmother, with her gorgeous white hair, fair skin and adorable smile, walking me as a very small girl of 6 or 7 with her little dog (on snowy days in Montreal) to the movies . . . the three movie buffs—pooch included—off together." She continued

..."My grandmother was also very beautiful—white hair and a dynamic sense of humor—and I was mad about her. The white-white of the gardenia with its sweet fragrance reminds me of those two marvelous ladies."

Nita is a Sunrise person. She has a wonderful sense of color and a cheerful home that reflects the sparkle of her palette—against, of course, a white background.

Ambiance:

Am-bi-ance: *A surrounding or pervading atmosphere; environment*

Each palette expresses a different mood. The French have a word for this (they usually do). They call it ambiance. Your answers to the quiz tell you, by looking back at the colortime you circled for question 2, where you will feel most in harmony with your surroundings. If you circled more than one colortime, simply choose the palette that best expresses the mood or ambiance you want to convey.

An environment done in the Sunrise colortime palette conveys a soothing and refreshing message, perfect for a summer porch filled with wicker or a place at the beach.

Sunset colors convey warmth and security. They are perfect for "lived-in" rooms such as a country kitchen, a den, a family room—ideally, a room with a fireplace.

Environments done in the Sunlight (Midday) colortime palette are inviting, easy to live with, and never overwhelming. The delicious ripe-fruit colors are often used in dining rooms and fine restaurants. They make a perfect compromise for people who share an environment but have differing color tastes. We explore this subject further in Chapter Three, "Using Color With Flair All Around You."

Remember that each colortime palette has both warm and cool colors, plus light, medium, and dark values of each of them, so there is enormous flexibility within each palette. If you have a really strong affinity for a certain colortime, you never have to leave it.

For example: if you're a strong PM person who chooses to do your house in the warm range of sunset colors, but want some cool tranquility in the bathrooms, you simply dip into the cool PM colors. These deep teals, antique turquoises, and greyed-blues are not as pure as the AM cools, but they will still impart a cool feeling, and you will find them far easier to live with than the AM blues and greens. And, as I mentioned before, you will be less likely to tire of your colortime cools because they relate so well to the other colors in your PM palette.

This is equally true for each of the colortime palettes. You can stay completely within the framework of your own colortime and still achieve the necessary variety. As a matter of fact, it's important to maintain a balance between warm and cool colors, regardless of the colortime you have selected.

If only cool colors are used in any one area, the mood can be chilling. To be complimented on the cool, serene ambiance of your house is one thing, but to be told that it seems cold would definitely not be a compliment!

Always observe this fundamental guideline: Cool colors should be balanced by a touch of warmth and warm colors by a touch of coolness. If you were to use only bright, warm colors in a room, that room could start to feel uncomfortably hot—especially in summer.

In a warm room, your eye will search for something cool for balance. In a cool room, your eye searches for a touch of warmth. But don't carry your balancing act too far—a combination of half-warm and half-cool simply doesn't work. It is far more esthetically pleasing to keep the cool colors dominant and the warm colors subordinate, or vice-versa. The rewards will be felt each time you enter that room.

Walter Scott, the renowned 20th Century-Fox set designer who has won many awards over the years, told me an intriguing story about an ambiance he created for **Barbra Streisand.** He was doing the sets for the film version of "Hello Dolly" and being the delightfully considerate man that he is, wanted to be sure that Barbra felt comfortable in her portable dressing rooms. He discovered that one of her favorite colors is a lovely dusty ash rose called "Bois de Rose."

He did the entire area in variations of that color, complete with leaded glass, creamy antique lace curtains, and accents of topaz, another Streisand favorite. He knew that Barbra loves Art Nouveau shadings and by combining the film's turn-of-the-century setting with "her" colors was able to keep the "Hello Dolly" mood alive for her both on and off camera. Barbra loved it. She is a strong PM person.

In her spacious New York apartment, she combined the ash rose and greyed-blues of her colortime in the formal living room. The library is a deep bordeaux accented with bronze accessories. Her bedroom is done in a deep lilac haze, rust, and evergreen. These highly unusual, interesting, and dramatic combinations reflect Barbra's individuality, creativity, and personal colortime. She feels very much at home there—just as you will feel when you are surrounded with the hues of your preferred colortime palette.

Walter is a definite AM individual. He does research in a den with mauve-taupe walls, where there is little to distract him from his work. Its ceiling is sky blue. When he needs to reflect on a thought, he tells me, he just looks up and is refreshed.

For contrast, and to relieve monotony, he uses sparkling red and yellow accents in pillows and paintings. He also uses Mexican tin and touches of shiny lacquer—two textures that are very complementary to an AM setting.

Come vacation time, Walter escapes to the water. Nothing is more restful and serene to him than to be surrounded by blue. Morning is his favorite time of day. There really is no question about the color-time that best mirrors his preferences.

Think of a place you don't like to visit and you'll probably come up with the dentist's office. One of my clients is a dentist whose motto is "gentle dentistry." How could we use anything else but the gentle, Midday colortime palette for her? We decided on soft mauve and powdered blues with wine carpeting. Even the equipment is done in soft, non-threatening colors. Soothing colors can be crucial in this sort of stressful environment. Calm patient and relaxed doctor equal gentle dentistry.

Another of my clients said that he never even notices the colors in his dentist's office—he's paralyzed when he goes in and numb when he comes out!

You may not think you're aware of color, but you truly are. The message may be subliminal, but it's always there to create an effect and to color your decisions, your moods, and your world.

The Crossovers Nature's Most Versatile Colors

Certain colors on the Color Clock are called crossover colors. Because these colors occur most frequently in nature, your eye is accustomed to seeing them in combination with many other colors.

The crossovers may be used with all of the colortime palettes. They're often used as background colors, either in combination with other colors, or in the same way a neutral color might be used.

Sky Blue

Did you ever look at a red geranium, a purple iris, or a yellow daffodil against the backdrop of a blue sky and think "What an awful color combination . . . Mother Nature really goofed!" Of course not. We're aware of the blue of the sky around us nearly every day. Blue skies far outnumber cloudy (or smoggy) days in most climates. As a result, our eyes and minds are accustomed to a blue backdrop for nature's myriad colors.

How can you take advantage of Mother Nature's favorite background color? Hang a painting with lots of blue sky as background in a room done in any of the three palettes. Not only will it not intrude, it can be an excellent way to bring a cool touch into a warm room for color balance.

Evergreen

Would you banish a fern from your living room because it clashed with the sofa?! When nature "arranges" flowers, green in the one color that appears in virtually every composition. Nature's greens are among the most versatile of hues, particularly shades of grass green, leaf green, forest green, and evergreen. When we're outdoors we're surrounded by green plants, trees, shrubs, and grass. Even in the midst of winter snows, faithful pine trees soften the stark landscape with graceful branches of green.

Sunlight Yellow

The clear yellow of sunlight permeates our atmosphere. Sunlight yellow works well as a neutral color. It is a good color to bring into a room done in cool colors, to give a touch of warmth. Sunlight yellow is shared by all colortime palettes.

Brown (Terre Brun)

The French call a certain brown "terre brun." The phrase sounds more elegant than "dirt brown," doesn't it? Yet dirt brown—the brown of the soil—is what it means. The varying earth tones associated with soil, tree bark, and woody plants are an integral part of nature's basic color scheme. Your eye is accustomed to these unobtrusive colors, which function marvelously well as neutral colors.

The term dirt brown is more likely to evoke thoughts of muddy dogs than beautiful flowers unless you're a gardening enthusiast who knows the potential for lush growth inherent in dark, rich soil. It's a brown that is difficult to describe as either warm or cool because it's a happy marriage of both undertones. But other browns and beiges have a decided warm or cool cast and look best when combined with colors in a particular colortime. They are shown with each palette in the color section.

Raisin
This is a very popular shade of brown. It is slightly purpled—the color of the fruit from which it is derived—and blends beautifully with all colortime palettes.

Aubergine
Aubergine is the French word for eggplant. Their adroit use of this deep purpled-maroon, especially in interior design, has made it a classic.

Deep Wine
The various names for this dignified, basic, darkest of the reds are often confusing; many of them are used interchangeably, and the colors of the wines themselves vary widely.

The deep, rich sample shown with the crossover colors on Plate O is the most versatile wine and flatters all colortime palettes.

Taupe (Greige)
This is the ideal neutral. "Fawn," "otter," and "mushroom" are often used to describe taupe. It combines beige and grey, and, as a result, blends well with all palettes Some taupes have a light yellow-green undertone and work best with the warm colors of each palette. Other taupes have a mauve undertone and work well with cool colors. The straight grey-beige color called "greige" is the most versatile neutral. "Sand" is often the name given to the lightest taupes.

Black

Black is the inevitable color. No matter what colors we are exposed to during the day, we are ultimately exposed to the black of night. Black is the ultimate in sophistication and spans all colortime palettes.

Grey

Grey appears as the first light of early dawn, often as an undertone to the blue skies of daylight, and adds depth to the deeper blue of dusk. When the sky is not blue, it is usually grey, and since grey days are less cheery than blue days, we often feel the need to add a touch of vivid color to grey to give it pizzazz. Grey runs the gamut from almost black to nearly white. Pearl grey, grey flannel, and charcoal work with every palette.

Navy

Dark navy blue is sometimes referred to as midnight blue. It is associated with black and the color of night. It is a familiar background color and the most universal of all basic colors.

True Red

This is the red that has both cool and warm undertones. It works well for all palettes, but needs to be deepened or used as an accent in the Midday palette.

Intimate Environments and Extended Environments

Of the many environments that surround you, that of your clothing and cosmetics is the most personal. It is called your "intimate environment." You choose clothing and cosmetic colors just as you do anything else in your environment—because you have an affinity for those colors and because they create a pleasing and comfortable atmosphere around you.

Your esthetic color sense—what you see—plays an important role in your wardrobe decisions, especially in terms of what you see in the mirror. If you have hair the color of burnished copper, one glance in the looking glass tells you how smashing you look in bronzes and peaches. And if your skin is sallow, no one should have to tell you to avoid chartreuse.

You may have really good "instincts" about your personal colors. You have learned how to read the reactions of others and you know when your choices are validated by a favorable comment—or no comment at all. After years of working with people and their color needs I have found that the eye really doesn't lie about flattering or unflattering personal colors. Let your Colortime Quiz be your guide. If you have any doubts at all, choose your clothing colors from the colortime that contains the colors of your skin, eyes, and hair. You will feel best when you look your best, and you will look your best when you feel your best . . . it is a completed circle.

One of the most compelling reasons for doing your wardrobe in your preferred colortime is that all of your clothing will blend and harmonize.

As you have learned, you don't judge color just by what you *see*. You also judge it by what you *feel*. The feeling part is very important and cannot be ignored. I could tell you until I am blue in the face that your best color is yellow-green because your eyes are yellow-green. But if your internal tape recorder goes on instant rewind to an unpleasant experience involving yellow-green, your recorder will eject my suggestion. I might be able to convince you otherwise, but your initial reaction would remain negative.

On the other hand, your initial reaction might be very positive. If Janet and Jamie have big, beautiful blue eyes, naturally Mommie dresses Janet and Jamie in blue. Every time they wear something blue, someone comments, "Oh look, the twins are in blue. Aren't they adorable." "Look at those two darling children in the blue sweaters. Don't they have beautiful blue eyes!"

So Janet and Jamie get compliments, approval, and "warm fuzzies" whenever they wear blue, and it feels good. Every time they look at something that is a Midday blue (the color of their eyes), a little bell rings in their internal tape recorders, signaling approval.

Their positive response to blue is reinforced by their awareness that blue skies mean they can go outside to play. Even as adults, the twins continue to respond to blue with pleasant feelings. You will learn more about your color associations in Part Two—"What Color Says About You."

The major portion of your personal environment extends to the world around you—your home and all of its furnishings, your office or place of business, your garden, your car. Color choices are of obvious importance because your extended environment is a reflection of you.

You want to be sure of these choices because they involve some of the biggest investments you will ever make. The Color Clock will give you the confidence to overcome old prejudices and open your mind to exciting new possibilities.

Understanding Undertones

To better understand the differences in the colortime palettes, think in terms of undertone. There are both warm and cool colors in all three palettes. Warm AM colors have an undertone of the rosy glow of sunrise. Warm PM colors have an undertone of the gold of sunset. The Midday colortime dips into both palettes, but never with a heavy hand.

For greatest harmony, colors blend best if they are in the same colortime palette. For example: shocking pink has a definite blue undertone (AM). Apricot is a light warm yellow-orange (PM). Shocking pink and apricot would not be a particularly pleasing combination because they are not in harmony. Paprika and apricot are more effective together, because they have the same yellow-gold undertones. They are both PM colors.

Cool AM colors are often "sharper" than PM colors. Imagine the electric blue-green of a tropic ocean in the morning. These are AM colors. Now picture the deeper blue of the ocean at dusk. You are now seeing PM colors. Next imagine that ocean at high noon. It is still a beautiful blue-green, but because of the sun's intensity, it appears a bit muted.

Another example of pleasing combinations from the same colortime palette is AM ruby with shell pink. If a third color were chosen to harmonize and you wanted to use a neutral tone, rose-beige would be the most effective because of its similar undertone.

Geranium and brick red are handsome PM colors. A blending neutral would be cream beige. A Midday combination of grape, mauve, and mushroom would be striking, yet subtle.

Purple, which blends red and blue, is a complex color. Redder, warmer purples blend best with the Sunset colortime. Cooler, bluer purples blend best with Sunrise. Lighter and deeper tones blend best with Sunlight colortime. It can be difficult to see how much red—or blue—undertone is in a particular purple.

If you're having "purple" trouble, use your color palette. If your palette is elsewhere, your eye will have to be your guide. If the color you're combining the purple with pleases your eye, go with it. Another trick for shopping when you don't have your palette with you is to compare similar colors. If you hold one purple against another (or compare any two similar colors), the undertone will pop right out at you. It's always best, of course, to try to keep your swatches with you, to be on the safe side.

Teal is a wonderfully versatile shade that flatters many skin types by bringing out the pink or peach of the skin. It is also a complex blend;

some teals are bluer, and some are greener. Check your color swatches to see which teal works best with the palette you are using.

If you love a color that doesn't appear in your favorite colortime, try it in a light-reflective fabric. The color will change according to the way the light either bounces off of it, or is absorbed by it, creating "hills and valleys" of variation. It will be more flattering than the same color would be in a dull, matte finish.

Mixing Palettes

As a general rule, colors from the Sunrise palette blend best when used together and colors from the Sunset blend best when used together. However, as with any rule, there is always the exception. The opposing Sunrise and Sunset palettes may be used together for deliberate discord or as attention-getters. This is a common technique in advertising, packaging, sign painting, and billboards.

You will often see colortime palettes combined in wallcoverings, furnishings, and carpeting in model homes. The reason for this is to make the house so memorable that long after you have forgotten how dramatic (or hideous) the combinations were, the home and location will stand out in your mind as something to remember.

If the effect is blaring, like the psychedelics of the 60's, it is called "discordant." Do you remember AM kelly green used with PM hot purple? If the effect is not hard on the eyes, it is called a "hybrid" combination. Cool AM purples and warm PM rusts are examples of hybrids that many designers have combined well, especially in intricate paisley prints.

Many combinations in the Sunlight colortime are examples of interesting, but subtle, hybrid blends. The Sunlight palette shares peach with the Sunset palette and mauve with the Sunrise palette. When used together, the unique combination of peach melba and mauve is very flattering to the mixtures found in the Sunlight colortime. They quietly claim your attention, but the more discordant mixtures of the Sunrise and Sunset palettes command it.

The illustrations in the color section show you some of the most attractive combinations in your colortime. Use them to help guide you in making your choices.

If you have an especially strong affinity for a particular colortime, you might be perfectly content never to leave it. And you may choose not to. But if you have an especially favorite color, and it's not in your preferred colortime palette, I would be the last person to advise you *never* to use it—never is a long, long time. It might evoke some wonderful childhood memory. If you always chose lemon gumdrops over every other flavor, you will remember the color as well as the taste. Lemon yellow brings back memories of delicious trips to the neighborhood candy store or a Saturday afternoon at the movies with your best friend.

If lemon yellow is not a part of your colortime palette, scatter a bit of that color through a room via accents or touches. You should always have a candy dish full of lemon gumdrops on hand to keep those happy memories alive—and maybe to create some special ones for *your* children to cherish!

The key to mixing colortime palettes successfully is to keep one palette dominant and the other subordinate. The dominant colortime palette should be 75 percent (or more) of the combination, and the subordinate colortime should be 25 percent (or less). You may vary this somewhat. Try 85 percent or 90 percent dominant. You'll find these proportions also work well. This system works for any combination involving two colors, even if they come from the same colortime.

Just as with music, discord is not always unpleasant, but our ears may tire of too much discordant sound. The same principle applies to color.

You may deliberately combine colortime palettes, but don't forget to do your math. Your eyes will tire of too much vibrant discord. And if your eyes get tired, you get tired, grumpy, and unsettled, and start looking for a change.

I have suggested that clients who want to experiment with a wild and crazy combination that equally combines two opposing palettes buy a beach towel or a pair of shorts. If you get tired of it, you haven't invested a fortune. But if you have gone to the expense of putting up new wallpaper and want to claw it off in three months, you're in trouble. Be careful when you decorate. Choose combinations that you can live with for a long time. Most of us simply can't afford the time, energy, or money to keep changing.

The most effective use of combined palettes I've ever seen was in the charming Georgetown home of a friend of mine in Washington, D.C. **Helen M.** was widowed at an early age. Her husband had been with the State Department, and they had traveled all over the world. She collected fabulous furnishings and had exquisite taste.

Helen loved the AM colors. She had a beautiful Oriental rug and she decorated her living room around it. The carpet's colors were wine, an off-white with a blue-pink undertone, and cool brown; distinctive touches of peacock blue shimmered throughout the design.

The walls were painted the same pinkish-white of the rug; Helen's marvelous antiques were of highly polished mahogany and cherry; and the luxurious velvet sofas echoed the rug's wine tones. Small touches of peacock blue appeared on two tiny provincial chairs by a bay window, and in the needlepoint and Persian tapestry pillows that graced the sofas.

The room was done predominantly in the AM palette. But Helen told me that she always had to have a touch of that wonderful PM peacock blue in every room of the house. The first time she showed me a picture of her husband, I knew exactly where her love of that color came from. Mr. M. had a kindly face, with the most iridescent greyed blue-green eyes I have ever seen. She will always associate that color with the happy years of her marriage.

Exploding Old Myths— White Does Not Go With Everything

Pure white is not a neutral color. It is dazzling and brilliant and impossible to ignore. It will not "go with everything." For decorating purposes, it is often necessary to add a touch of another shade or tint as an undertone to white paint to cut the glare that white generates. In an office or work environment, it is extremely important to control glare to reduce eye strain. Off-white is a more effective neutral.

Because it is so highly reflective, especially in a fabric with a sheen, pristine white acts as a mirror as it reflects the color used immediately next to it. For example, if you use orange checks on a white background, the white will warm up slightly, because the orange is so warm. Bright colors are slightly dulled next to pure white.

Mixing whites never works. Off-whites will look dull and dingy next to pure white. Your beautiful antique lace curtains will look yellowed and faded next to a snow-white shade. Super-sheer white fabrics, such as scrim curtains, disclose the color behind them, so they appear less white than a heavier texture would.

The AM colortime palette can use pure whites better than the PM or Midday, but a bit of blue-pink, light blue, or grey as an undertone would help to reduce glare.

In a Midday environment, a bit of any pastel, depending on the other colors in the room, makes a good undertone to white.

If you are using PM colors in the room, it would be best to add a tiny bit of yellow, gold, or beige, depending on the depth of the shade desired. This would give a slightly creamy cast and would blend best with the other PM colors.

White reflects into adjacent areas, which makes it excellent to use near darkened spaces. Pure white enlarges any area in which it is used, so when decorating your bed or your body, remember that anything amply upholstered will look larger in white!

Frank Westmore, of the famous family of makeup artists, told me that he discovered the enlarging effect of pure white when he was working on the film, "Geisha Girl," with **Shirley MacLaine.** He used the traditional white makeup and, as he put it, "Shirley's face looked like the moon!" In order to "save face," he added a bit of pink as an undertone to the stark white, which visually reduced the size of her face so that she no longer looked distorted. One of Japan's leading cosmetic houses now uses Frank's formula.

In clothing, a white sheer or semi-sheer fabric becomes an off-white. The undertone of the skin comes through and mutes the whiteness somewhat, making it a better choice for midday or PM skin tones. AM skin wears pure white best.

The glare from a white shirt or blouse can make the face look pale. Women can compensate for this by wearing more makeup, unless they have very pink, very dark, or very olive skin, which provides good contrast to white in the AM palette. If you love pure white, and you have a Midday or PM skin tone, save it for summer when your skin is tan. Many of my clients in those colortimes tell me they only wear white in summer, when the tan of the skin reflects into the white and makes it more becoming. If you're a Midday or PM with dark skin, you can wear pure white year round, but cream white or vanilla will blend best with the other shades of your palette.

Pure white is also at its best at night, when there are softening shadows. For Midday and PM men, crossover sky blue, light yellow, sand, and light grey are usually more flattering than pure white shirts. The AM skin may also wear those tints, since they are crossovers.

Regardless of fashion's whims, pure white stockings look too stark. A subtle sand is better. As for men—save your white socks for the tennis court.

Kay Sarazin, dynamic Hollywood hair coloring expert, travels all over the world demonstrating coloring techniques. She loves to wear dazzling white on stage because it is so luminous and attention-getting. These qualities give pure white preferred status with many performers. But if you have PM coloring, as Kay does, dranatize your makeup and add color to your face so that you won't look pale or sallow when you wear white. Kay always analyzes her clients' colortimes to be sure that the hair color is just right. You'll learn more about hair and makeup color in the next chapter.

Chapter 2

Making The Color Clock Tick For You

Putting Colors Together Successfully

One of the greatest challenges of working with color is to combine colors effectively and attractively. Choosing a single color to use is much easier than deciding what goes with what.

Most of the old color rules have disappeared. Using blues with greens was once considered in terrible taste, and combining red with pink was a no-no. The only rule today is "Never say Never." Think in terms of guidelines rather than rules, which can hamper your creativity and take the fun out of being open to new ideas. Guidelines can give you the confidence to know how—and what—to combine.

The simplest and safest way to combine colors is to stay within the borders of the colortime you have chosen to use. The formulas that professional designers use can provide you with the "know-how." Mastering them can help you to create terrific combinations.

All color formulas are based on the color wheel shown on Plate V. The Color Clock is designed to help you make happy marriages between harmonious and compatible colors. Of the many guidelines for color coordination, here are the least complicated and easiest to understand:

Harmonious Relations— **Analagous Colors**

All colors are derived from the primary hues of red, yellow, and blue. If you mix equal parts of two of these primaries, you get the secondary colors of orange, green, and purple. They are color kin. Orange is the child of yellow and red. Purple results from the union of red and blue. Each of the secondary colors has a harmonious relationship with its "parent" colors.

If you use green, yellow, and blue together (or orange, yellow, and red, or purple, red and blue), you have what is called a related or analagous color scheme.

The color wheel shows you the colors that are most closely related; these provide some of the easiest color schemes to work with. They are also the least apt to offend. These schemes are based on adjacent colors—yellow, yellow-orange, orange, and orange-red, for example, which share the same undertone.

If you want to expand your color "family," you can add a cousin from either the yellow-green side or the red side.

When you add these extra colors to clothing choices, they're best kept within the confines of a print; if used as separate colors, the relatives may get a little noisy as they vie for attention.

It is difficult to make a mistake with rooms done in related colors whose undertones are in the same colortime. If you want to be a bit more daring, try an expanded analagous combination. Rooms done in these colors occasionally need areas of solid black, white, or grey for definition, or a touch of pattern to avoid monotony.

Thank You For The Complement

Com-ple-ment: that which completes or makes perfect. Complementary or contrasting colors are those directly across from each other on the standard color wheel. They are called complements because they complete each other. Green, for example, is the complement to red, and never looks greener than when it is next to red. Conversely, red appears reddest when next to green. A red rose seems even redder against a green leaf.

Orange complements blue, and yellow complements purple. I was finally convinced that Elizabeth Taylor actually does have violet eyes when I saw her at the Academy Awards in bright daffodil yellow chiffon. When used in the brightest intensities, complementary colors are instant "zing" and can be real show-stoppers. The complementary color effect is a major reason for advising redheads to wear green.

Complementary combinations can be super-dramatic, but can also be strident in their call for attention. People with outgoing personalities often love them. When designers package products, they frequently use the brightest intensities of complementary colors. On your next trip to the market, look at the brilliant array of detergent boxes all begging for your attention. Notice how many are done in the sharpest complementary combinations.

Complementaries can be used to wonderful advantage, but can also boomerang. If your skin flushes easily and you have a ruddy complexion, bright green next to your face will bring out the pink (light red) in your skin. The green should be lightened or deepened for a more flattering effect. When the intensity of one or both of the complementaries is muted, the combination is much easier on the eyes. For example, a shocking AM pink and deep emerald green combination is less jarring optically than the same shocking pink when paired with kelly green. When you are looking for a gasoline station, that oscillating orange and brilliant blue ball above the station can be spotted easily. Deepening the orange to a PM rust and combining it with a greyed deep blue from the same colortime would probably sell less gasoline, but the colors would be easier to live with. You can soften the shock of complementaries by choosing unexpected tints and shades of the two colors.

It is best to stay within your colortime when using complementaries so that your eye will not tire of combinations quickly. If you do combine palettes, use only a touch of the subordinate colortime. Remember our dominance and subordination guideline: one color is always the star and takes center stage, while the other is the supporting player.

For example: In a PM room of paprika and hunter green, the walls and mini-blinds might be hunter green with accents of lighter green in plants and accessories. The area rug, chair pads, and place mats are paprika against a warm pine dining table and chairs. Green is the dominant color, paprika the subordinate. (The pine set is treated as a neutral because it is unobtrusive, but its warmth blends with the PM colors.)

When intense or strongly contrasting colors are offset by neutral colors, the combination becomes much richer. The neutrals enhance the brighter colors by making them easier to view. For example: Vivid AM orchid dawn and daybreak yellow might be great fun in a Hawaiian print shirt, but when these hues are subtly mixed with grey, taupe, or beige, the combination gains both elegance and a quiet neutral shade to use as an accessory color.

What To Do If Your Chair (Or Hair) Is Fading

As you follow the circle of the color wheel, think of your own coloring. Complementary colors in your colortime can help to keep you from fading away, (as we all do to some extent with age). Blue eyes are enhanced by browns, raisins, oranges, and corals. Green eyes are flattered by wines, pinks, and reds. Hazel eyes are chameleons that pick up and reflect many of the colors that are worn near them. They often combine many colors, but one color usually predominates. Complementary colors are very effective with hazel eyes and can virtually change their color.

Brown eyes and hair are complemented by greens, especially blue-greens. Since grey is a neutral, it really doesn't have a complementary color as such, but it is enhanced by touches of color. Neither does black have a true complement, but both bright hues and white contrast effectively with it.

If you are blonde, purpled shades and tints will make you look blonder. As we have noted, green is often suggested for redheads, but bright blues are actually more complementary because "red" hair is closer to orange than to red.

The color wheel in the color section illustrates the complementary colors.

Complementary colors can be used very effectively in interiors. A large painting with blue sky in the background can be a perfect foil for the coppery carpet of a PM room. Wallpaper laced with leafy greens may be just the antidote to the tired pink tiles and plumbing fixtures of a once-bright AM bathroom.

If your AM blue chair is fading in a bright, sunny room, a pillow with a touch of orange—but just a touch—may restore its vitality. In a Midday room, soften the orange to melon. If your celadon chair is disappointingly dull, use something around it, on it, or under it that contains red, rose, or wine, and watch it come alive. If you are using the Midday palette, the softer complementaries will be more pleasing.

Monochromatics

A monochromatic color scheme uses only one hue in varying shades and tints. The secret of a successful monochromatic scheme is to select all of the variations of this single hue from the same colortime in order to avoid clashing undertones.

If you are working with varying shades of AM blue-red, for example, those from seashell pink to ruby red look best together because they have the same blue undertone. A good PM red combination would be brick red with honeyed corals. An attractive Midday combination would be dusty rose and strawberry cream.

Weddings are excellent occasions for being creative with mono-chromatic color schemes. The mother of the bride can be lovely in varying tones of an AM aquamarine with undertones from the same colortime. When I coordinate wedding parties, I often suggest that everyone wear monochromatic colors from the same colortime. It's much easier to choose flowers, the wedding pictures are lovely because everyone's colors blend so well, and a beautiful occasion becomes even more beautiful.

In monochromatic color schemes, light and bright shades and tints draw the eye first. So unless you want your feet to be the focal point, use darker colors at the lower part of your body and lighter and brighter shades as you move toward your face, which then becomes the focal point.

In the case of the bride's mother, who plans to wear aquamarine crepe with an overlay of chiffon, the aqua tones of the top of the dress would gradually deepen towards the hem. Her shoes would be a slightly deeper shade than the hem. If she chose to wear a flower in her hair, it should be as light as, or lighter, than the top of her dress. Darkening the colors at the lower part of the body gives stability to the figure, makes it appear slimmer, and directs attention to the face.

The ultimate monochromatic color scheme uses only one color with very little variation. The effect can be quite stark or even severe, but it is very dramatic. Using a variety of textures and shapes can help to avoid too much sameness.

I recently received a call for help from a woman who had done her apartment's entire living/dining area in beige. The contemporary room was well done and quite comfortable, but she was starved for color. Rather than interrupt the wonderful lines of the furniture and the flow of the room—and because she lived in a mild climate—I suggested that she keep banks of colorful potted plants and flowers on the balcony, which could be seen through the sliding glass doors.

Most of her furniture faces the balcony and she simply changes the pots with the seasons to whatever flowers in her favorite colortime are then in bloom. At night, spotlights illuminate the greenery and she feels as though she lives in a garden, even though she is in the heart of a big city.

Neutral Territory

Neutral colors can make very effective monochromatic combinations, but they can also be tricky. It's usually not too difficult to find tan pants, a camel corduroy jacket, and a beige sweater with the same undertones. But finding appliances and tile in matching or blending undertones is a real challenge. It is, however, well worth the effort. Your colortime samples can help you avoid expensive mistakes in undertone.

Have you ever bought a shirt in bone to go with slacks of the same color only to get home and find that they don't go together at all? Or found beige grasscloth as the perfect background for your beige sofa and then discover that the colors don't even come close? Although it is not necessary to find colors that match perfectly (it's better to look for a blend than a match because dye lots are never exactly the same), undertones should always blend. Straw baskets, wicker, hemp, and macrame are useful natural elements that can blend into almost any background.

Grey is another great neutral that lends itself well to monochromatic combinations. There are warm PM greys and cool AM greys, but the most versatile greys of all are the balanced, crossover Pearl and Grey Flannel, and charcoal. These are the greys that blend with every colortime. (See examples in Crossover Colors.)

Terrific Taupe

Taupe is the neutral that gets the gold star for versatility. It is the happy union of beige and grey, with several different undertones. A pinkish mauve undertone works with most AM colors. A golden (and sometimes greenish) undertone works with most PM colors. The best taupe for the Midday palette is a medium grey-beige, often named "mushroom," with neutral, barely discernible undertones.

Because of their versatility and the fact that they are actually a blend of two neutrals, all taupes are crossover colors. I suggest the warm taupe for blending with the warm colors in all colortimes, and the cool mauve taupe for blending with the cool colors in all colortimes. The crossover middle-value taupe known as greige blends with all colortimes. It is also called "otter," and "fawn." The lighter crossover taupe called "sand" is also a terrific neutral taupe. Once you discover taupe (if you haven't yet), you'll wonder how you ever managed without it.

People who like the Midday palette best have a strong affinity for neutral colors, especially in interiors, perhaps because they recognize how well neutrals complement the muted ice-cream tints of Midday.

Jean Donahue, a Studio City, California interior designer, makes interesting use of taupe and other neutrals. She relies heavily on the Color Clock when planning interiors for homes, offices, and theatres.

In her own home, which has been featured in films and television commercials, Jean has artfully combined evergreen, peach melba, and taupe. Her personal colortime is in the Midday palette.

Neutral colors are excellent budget stretchers because they blend well, are basic and dependable, are not trendy, never offensive, and make excellent background colors. They are also marvelous foils for bright accents. It is much easier on the bank account to use temporarily tempting colors in accents like silk flowers, pillows, and lampshades. Such accessories cost relatively little and can be changed much more easily than large pieces.

Accent colors may come and go according to what is "in," but a neutral background conveys a feeling of permanence and style.

Duochromatics

A duochromatic combination consists of just two colors. There are also two basic guidelines to remember here: The first is that the eye will be drawn to the area where the two colors meet. A dark bathing suit may make your figure appear smaller, but it will also draw attention to the upper thigh, where the light color of the skin meets the dark of the suit, or vice-versa. If you are chunkier than you'd like to be, a bathing suit that matches your skin tone is more flattering because it blends with your body and presents no line of demarcation to draw the eye.

The second guideline again focuses on the basic math of one dominant and one subordinate color—75 percent or slightly more of one shade and 25 percent or less of another.

These proportions are less distracting than equal divisions of color. For example: A navy suit with red shoes, red bag, red sweater, and red hat would be much too busy. The eye is drawn to too many areas at once and you don't know where to look first.

A better choice would be to make the suit, since it already covers so much area, the dominant color. The shoes should be navy, the bag could be navy with red trim. The sweater could stay red, but the hat would be better in a patterned combination of navy and red. Attention would then be brought to the face, making it the focal point.

The effectiveness of duochromatics can be in the simplicity of combining just two colors. Just as with monochromatics, one or both of the colors may vary in value or intensity. For example: Crossover shades of dark and light grey, used with aubergine and a touch of mauve, would be considered a duochromatic combination, but would offer more variety than straight grey and aubergine with no variations. Complementary combinations could also be considered duochromatic, but are only those that oppose each other on the color wheel.

A duochromatic combination may be very dramatic in its simplicity. A traditional example is black and white. Black is a crossover color. If you are a stickler for precision, blue-black is specifically AM, umber black is PM, and the Midday is a combination of both. But it is splitting hairs to try to differentiate between them and I never suggest that my clients run around searching for just the right black.

Finding similar undertones in black only becomes important when you are combining blacks in the same outfit. We've all had the experience of putting a black sweater with black pants only to discover that the blacks looked awful together. They were from different colortimes.

It is less critical to match blacks in a room setting than it is in clothing. In interiors, you are apt to use a variety of textures together and colors and textures are more widely spaced than they are in clothing. The best combinations of black and white are black and pure white for AM; black and cream white for PM; and black and vanilla for Midday.

The most dramatic use of black and white I have ever seen was at a party given after the premiere of a film at a major film studio. (The picture was terrible, but the party was terrific.)

The tables were done in black tablecloths with white place settings and tapering white candles. White camellias, gardenias, mums, tulips, and roses, in single-faceted crystal bud vases of various heights, were placed on gleaming mirrors on the center of each table. Everything sparkled and glimmered. It was truly breathtaking.

Each of the guests was asked to wear black or white. The men wore black tuxes with gleaming white shirts, and the women wore long black or white gowns. One of the most incredibly beautiful women I have ever seen was there that night. **Merle Oberon** wore a black taffeta gown which, with her flawless AM white skin, carried out the evening's motif perfectly. Whenever I see her in the original version of *Wuthering Heights* (which I've probably seen about 50 times and I still cry buckets), I think about that wonderful party.

Simple, unadorned, stark black can be fabulous in clothing whenever it provides strong contrast, such as on redheads, blondes, or silver- or white-haired wearers in any colortime. It is also wonderful on fair or rosy AM skin, light creamy PM skin, and the ivory skin of Midday. For the rest of us, black needs a touch of pizazz near the face, such as a hint of red in a patterned tie, or the contrast of a light or brightly colored shirt.

Trichromatics

A trichromatic color scheme uses three colors. One color dominates (approximately 70 percent), the second is subordinate (20 percent), and the third is used as just a touch (10 percent). This third color can be used effectively to draw the eye to a given area, making it a focal point. If you were cooking, you'd call it a "pinch."

If a duochromatic room has become a bit tired, adding a third color for accent is a good way to revitalize it. A living room done in PM deep teal and dusk blue could be perked up with coral dust pillows. An accent color should be used more than just once—you might repeat the coral dust as emphasis in a print or in some other accessory piece.

When dressing in classic grey flannel and pearl, such as in a suit with a shirt, wine is an excellent highlighting accent—as in a wine and two-tone grey scarf or tie.

By placing the third color in the scarf or tie, you draw attention to the face. If you were to add this accent in a belt, the waist becomes the focal point. Use the accent color wherever it is the most flattering.

If your legs aren't as shapely as you'd like them to be, or your feet are bigger than you like them to be, don't wear an accent color in your shoes, particularly in bright tones and most particularly in white. White is a brilliant color, and enlarging. Dazzling white is okay on a tennis court, but white needs to connect with a predominantly white outfit or white pants. With other AM colors, pure white can look crisp and clean in the summer, or in the tropics, but, as I have pointed out, white is not a neutral and cannot go with everything. So ignore that old "It's summer and I must have white shoes to go with everything" routine. If you're not using AM colors, you don't need white at all. Taupe is really smarter for all colortime palettes—even when worn with white. You especially don't want white shoes to blink on and off under a darker outfit.

One particular three-color combination is called "triadic." This plan uses three equidistant colors on the standard color wheel. A conventional triadic scheme of navy, true red, and a sliver of yellow might appear on the comfortable plaid sofa in Dad's den. These are all crossover colors that have wide appeal for all colortimes, especially for men.

The same scheme could be adapted for a child's room in a crayola combination of AM bright blue, cherry red, and cheerful daybreak yellow. A Midday scheme in this triad might be china blue, dusty rose, and banana. A triadic PM possibility would be dusk blue, bordeaux, and harvest gold.

Polychromatics

When a combination includes more than three colors, it is referred to as polychromatic. The combining of more than three solid hues can seem very "spotty" and the eye is often distracted. Yet groups of colors can be combined effectively both in clothing and in interiors. Prints, plaids, and tweeds often successfully mix many more than three colors.

Polychromatic schemes are most harmonious when one hue, such as the background color, is predominant. For example, a sofa of multifloral printed linen in the southwestern desert PM shades of terra cotta (background), cream, apricot, and antique turquoise, with a touch of harvest gold, might be used against terre cotta walls. Cream suedecloth chairs as accessories and a carpet of antique turquoise would complete the scheme. Terra cotta becomes the predominant color because it occupies the largest area.

You might feel more comfortable using the harvest gold as the carpet color and it would probably be the most popular color choice for this particular combination. Gold is extremely versatile, blends well with many colors, and gives a feeling of warmth to a room. But the antique turquoise would provide greater contrast and be more distinctive. Either is "correct." They are both in the same PM colortime. It's simply a matter of personal choice.

Crossover sunlight yellow is shared equally by all colortimes. Gold in fabric is actually a PM color, but is a mellowed yellow that shares many of the same qualities of sunlight yellow yet is a bit more subtle. If you have moved into a home or an apartment where the carpeting is gold and you want to use AM or Midday colors against it, it won't be too objectionable because of gold's relationship to crossover yellow.

In clothing, a typical polychromatic combination for either men or women would be donegal wool tweed with a crossover medium grey background interspersed with tiny random flecks of navy, wine, and evergreen. Any of these colors would work in a blouse or shirt. For men in a conservative business setting, however, a lighter grey shirt with a navy or wine tie would be most appropriate.

Instant Irritants and Dramatic Discord

For color at its most harmonious, avoid using opposite colortime palettes of AM and PM *in equal amounts* in the brightest intensities. They will fight for attention on your body, and in a room they will look overdone, busy, and just plain uncomfortable or irritating. Combining the sparkling jewel tones of the AM with the fiery tones of the PM can be tiresome and even tacky.

If the kids spend too much time in the bathroom, try equal amounts of a strong AM fuchsia and a PM burnt orange in a big floral print, and they'll get out in a hurry. The only problem is that you won't want to stay in there either. A client's husband threatened to paint the spare bedroom in a thoroughly obnoxious combination of colors if any more relatives came to visit. He told me that he gave up on the idea when he realized that his in-laws would probably love it!

Discord can be very dramatic if used in the right proportions. Various tones of earthy bronze and warm PM beiges could have a smidgin of sapphire blue thrown in to gain attention, and a dash of cool regal purple against a PM cinnamon is certainly different and dramatic. Discord isn't always ugly if you follow the guidelines of dominance and subordination. But it's not for the faint-hearted or basically practical person.

It takes a talented designer with a real flair for color to use odd or highly unusual combinations, but you can create unusual combinations within your colortime and not run the risk of looking eccentric.

What if somebody gives you a gift that is a discordant combination of colors? You may not particularly like it, but if your brand new mother-in-law gives it to you, you feel you have to show up in it. Let's assume that it's a bulky (and itchy) wool V-necked cardigan in her (not your) favorite shades of horizon purple. You are a Midday and really are not turned on at all to those particular purples. They make your complexion kind of grey (nauseous green might come closer). What can you do?

If you wear a plaid cotton shirt with the collar out of the V-neck, it will not only solve the itchies, it will also do what I call "breaking the color line." Allowing other colors next to your face to reflect in your hair, skin, and eyes keeps the purple from being right up under your chin. The shirt might have a single line of purple running through the plaid; the other colors could be softened Midday colors such as mauve, vanilla, and lilac.

The small amount of purple in the shirt would blend with the sweater—remember that it doesn't have to match perfectly. The other colors will all be in your colortime so you have a happy solution.

Phyllis Diller has made fantastic use of discord in what she calls her "wild colors." She says she loves "sparkling, unheard-of combinations"... and that shocking pink is her best performing color. True red is wonderful and "up," but wine is a bit "down." Forget purple and black for Phyllis—they depress her.

She really does have an excellent color sense and interestingly enough, in her off-stage hours, prefers the light colors, especially monochromatic beiges and grey in clothing.

Bette Midler assembles some of the zaniest discordant combinations for the stage—all done with a wonderfully tacky flair. But in her civilian hours, she retreats into the more subdued combinations of her PM palette.

Many people, when they choose clothes, are confused about what goes with what in accessories because trends change so rapidly. In order to make your choices easier, I've listed the following guidelines:

For Women Only: Shoes

A good "when in doubt" guideline is to keep shoe colors the same tone as your hemline, or make them a deeper shade. At one time in fashion, it was the only way to go. Now there are some exceptions to this rule:

1. When you wear pants, shoes are not as outstanding as they are with a skirt or a dress because an elongated line is created through the leg. But let your eye be the judge. If shoes are too bright, light, white, or shiny, they may be distracting and bring the eye to the feet first (you don't want your feet to be a focal point, especially if you're self-conscious about your shoe size).

2. When wearing over-the-calf (not short) boots, the leg appears elongated, so it is not necessary to match the hemline.

However, the figure is lengthened even more when the hemline and boot do match. For an even longer line, match stockings to boots.

3. Boots could blend, match, or relate to something in the top of the outfit. For example: A crossover plaid shirt of true red, navy, and evergreen with jeans and red boots.

4. When wearing a light-to-medium value or neutral color, neutral shoes work best. They may be somewhat lighter, darker, or the same tone as the hemline. For example: a PM coral dress with light camel shoes, or an AM orchid dress with grey shoes.

Taupe is definitely the most versatile of all neutrals, since it goes with almost all colors, except for very dark shades. Which brings us to our next guideline.

5. Very dark hues in an outfit do need dark shoe colors. Black, navy, dark purple, wine, raisin, charcoal grey, deep evergreen, aubergine, brown, etc. need to be supported by dark shoes. Neutral shoes would be too light. In fashion, this is called stability—the balancing of the darker shades on the upper body with those of the lower body. This is especially important to anyone whose proportions are wider below than they are above. The most versatile of all the dark accessory colors for shoes are the crossover shades of wine, aubergine, and raisin. They blend with more shades than black does.

6. Shoes may be dyed to match, especially when the color is unusual. This is usually a very dramatic or fun approach, but it's not absolutely necessary. If you like to "play" with colors, experiment on an older pair of shoes in fairly good condition. A deep emerald green long dress might be beautiful with matching shoes (if you can get them to match!), but strippy black sandals would work, too, and be far more practical.

7. Silver metallics look best with cool colors and gold works best with warm colors.

Stockings

A good rule of thumb is to blend the color of your stockings with the color of your shoes. It makes you look "leggier," and it's especially sexy in neutrals such as taupe. Models and actresses like **Lauren Bacall** often use this look on stage.

If you're the trendy type and want to use light stockings when they're in style, use something light at the top of the body, such as a blouse, a scarf, a collar, or jewelry as a connecting link to your face and to create good balance.

Dark stockings do not always make your legs look slimmer and light stockings do not always make your legs look heavier. It depends strictly on how you put the look together. Navy stockings under a light grey skirt will draw the eye directly to the point where the two colors come together and enlarge the legs by creating a horizontal line, but light sand stockings under a sand skirt create a longer line, especially when coordinated with sand shoes.

These are the basic "families" of stocking colors. Trends come and go, but these are the classic combinations:

1. TAUPE—This is the grey-beige "when in doubt" shade that blends with so many clothing colors. It's at its best with taupe and shades of grey or green. It is also a good shade when you'd rather not wear anything too dark with blacks and browns.

2. BEIGE TO MEDIUM BROWN—These shades go best with bone, off-white, tans, etc. Be careful to choose the proper undertones. Generally, the AMs are cooler, PMs warmer; Midday is a combination of the two. Cool pinky AM beige stockings would be horrendous with a warm PM camel beige shoe. Your legs would look as if they had turned red. If you are in doubt about colortime, compare several shades and you will see the undertones. Your colortime swatches may also help.

3. GREY TO OFF-BLACK—Best with grey and black, also possible with navy. Avoid beige with grey or black.

4. NEUTRAL—The best way to describe a neutral stocking is to say that it matches your skin shade. This is the stocking to wear when you want your leg color to be as unobtrusive as possible. For example: A slinky red dress with matching shoes makes enough of a statement without red stockings, too. Neutral hose would also be worn with white shoes.

5. WINE, AUBERGINE, and RAISIN—Outfits in these crossover colors need stockings that blend.

6. VERY DARK AND VERY LIGHT—Trend colors, such as pastels, dark or bright opaques will change according to the latest fashion. The general guideline is to blend to your shoe color, but for a fun look, blend to a color in the top of your outfit.

Handbags

Remember when handbags had to match shoes? Now the key word is "mood." As long as they are both sporty or dressy, forget all the old rules. The bag may still match your shoes, but it could also be lighter or somewhat darker, as long as the undertone is similar.

The neutral color is the most favored, practical way to go, most especially in taupe. Your bag may also match something in the body of the outfit, such as a belt, or it may be in a pattern that blends with your shoes or outfit.

Belts

Belts can be an interesting color accent. They may match your shoes, your bag, or a color in the body of your outfit, or they may blend with other accessories like jewelry or scarves. A belt will draw attention to the waist if its color contrasts with the background. That same color should be repeated in one or two additional spots on the body. Remember, a solid accent color should be used in no more than three places on the body or the look becomes spotty and distracting.

Jewelry

Since there are warm and cool colors in all palettes, silver and gold have a place in each colortime. The type of finish determines where it looks best. Shiny silvers and platinums work well with the cool AM jewel tones, and shiny gold with the warm AM tones. There are more warm colors in the PM, so Florentine golds and deep coppers complement the warm tones; and pewters, brushed, and antique silver look best with cool PM colors. Middays may use either, but favor the delustered finishes.

Gold is the equivalent of sunlight yellow and blends with all palettes. Silver and gold can be worn together, but it is best to keep the finishes compatible, such as brassy gold with shiny silver or brushed gold with antiqued silver.

White, bright fresh water pearls look best against AM colors or complexions. Creamy natural pearls work best against PM colors or complexions. Again, Midday people may choose either, depending on the undertones of the colors they are wearing.

Precious stones and gems are so highly reflective that they often blend with or pick up surrounding shadings. Iridescent stones such as opals seem to change according to available light, just as fabrics with a sheen do.

Some stones are so definite in their deep, bright, greyed, or honeyed intensity that they look best with other definite AM, Midday, or PM colors. For example, a dazzlingly bright aquamarine with a matching or blending AM tone, or melony coral with soft Midday values. Amber and topaz are usually PM preferences. Let your eye be your guide. At one time greys were only worn with silver. Now we see gold against charcoal and it looks marvelous. Except for a rare or unusual stone, or a very flawed stone, diamonds are so highly reflective that they work with everything—the perfect "crossover" jewel!

Cosmetics and Colors

The Color Clock can save you money by helping you choose the right cosmetic shade every time you buy. As every woman knows, it is easy to accumulate a drawerful of rejects—the makeup base that turned out to be the wrong shade and made you look like you were wearing a mask, or the lipstick that looked terrific on your best friend but just didn't make it on you.

Expensive mistakes like this can add up—a lot of money can go down the tube along with the lipsticks. I always recommend trying before buying. Certain shades look totally different on the skin than they do in the container. And sometimes a reaction to body chemistry (oiliness, ruddy tones, sallowness, etc.) will change a shade after it has been on the skin for a while.

Always try to buy cosmetics after you've been able to keep them on for a time. Ideally, the products should be applied first, as they are in a demonstration. This is the best way to go—you're unhurried, relaxed, and have a chance to see what the finished product looks like. Try to check yourself in daylight. If it isn't possible, then be sure to use good lighting.

There is nothing mysterious about choosing the correct cosmetic colors. The guidelines that follow can take the guesswork out of it. If you're like most of my clients, you buy too many colors and invariably go back to using your old reliable favorites. Chances are, these favorites are in your personal colortime and that's why you like them. But to help you avoid expensive mistakes (there are no more inexpensive mistakes), remember these pointers when you choose your most basic cosmetics:

1. Every colortime palette has both warm and cool colors, even though the AM tones are predominantly cool, PM tones predominantly warm, and Midday a balance of both. You simply need two "sets" of basics—lipstick, blush, and nail polish—one in the warm range of your colortime, and the other in its cool tones. If you're in the AM colortime and use many of the cool colors, you will still need a warmer tone to wear with the daffodil and daybreak yellows, rose-pink corals, and cocoa browns. PM people will use up their warm colors first, but need a cool tone to wear with blues, greens, and purples. Middays are likely to make equal use of their warm and cool tones.

Use your colortime palette as a guide in choosing your shades. Don't try to match your palette perfectly; simply look for a blend. If your lipstick turns blue no matter what you wear (many people have that problem), try a yellow lipstick under it. If your lips go orange, try a flesh tone as an undercoat.

2. One basic makeup base should blend with your skin tone. Match it as closely as possible so that it doesn't look mask-like. You will have to do a lot of experimenting, but it's worth it to get the right shade. Use a colorless, translucent powder over any makeup shade so that the base color doesn't change.

3. Eye shadow colors can vary—your choices include:

a. The color of the undertones in your eyes, such as teal shadow with blue-green eyes, or amber with brown eyes.

b. A complementary color that intensifies the color of your eyes, such as taupe for blue eyes, or a dusty rose for green eyes. The color wheel illustration on Plate V can help you to choose complementary shades, which are suggested by many cosmetic companies. The brightest shade of your "opposite" eye colors on the color wheel would be too intense, so you would need to darken or lighten it.

c. You might want to match your eye shadow color to your outfit. A very special color, say a dusty lilac, can be dramatically accentuated with a blending eye shadow.

Let your colortime colors guide your choice of eye shadow colors. Keep your shadow subtle. Dust it down with some taupe or grey so that it shadows, not overshadows your eyes. Basic mascara colors are black for dark lashes, dark brown for light lashes. Navy is good for blue-eyed people.

The following chart contains some color names to help you make your choices. Shades, of course, vary with the manufacturer. These are simply descriptive terms to help you differentiate between the three colortime palettes. If you have the kind of skin tone that defies every rule, you might have to experiment more than most.

Sunrise (AM)

Most bases in your colortime will have a very fair or slightly rose-pink or rose-brown undertone. If the base becomes too pink on the skin, go to a straight beige or brown with no discernible undertone and add your color by using blusher on your cheeks, chin, and forehead (just a touch). This is far better than using a shade that is so different from your skin tone that it creates a mask-like line of demarcation.

AM make-up base shades have names like:

Rose-Beige   Rose-Brown

| Cool Beige | Cocoa |
| Light Beige | Fair |

Blushers, rouges, lipsticks, glosses, and nail polishes will often have a blue-pink, rose-brown or rose-wine cast. The name will often tell you where to classify the color in the clock. Typical names include:

Ruby Red	Iced Mauve
Wine and Roses	Porcelain Rose
Sea Shell	Cherry Brown
Glazed Pink	Frosted Lavender
Rose Coral	

Adjectives used to describe gems are often a clue to AM shades. They are called: "icy," "glistening," "gleaming," "glossy," "glazed," "crystal," "diamond," "sparkling," "frosted," "super-frosted," "silvered," or "brightest."

Sunset (PM)

PM complexions will have a warm undertone. If there is any pink in the skin, it is warm and peachy—not the rosy pink of AM. Honey, cream, and golden are often used as adjectives to describe PM make-up base shades, which have names like:

Warm Beige	Rachel
Creamy Beige	Deep Tan
Honey Beige	Coffee Bronze
Peach	Amber

PM blushers, rouges, lipsticks, glosses, and nail polishes have tones of warm pink (such as coral), browned burgundy, golden brown and other tawny tones. These Sunset colors are often called:

Brandied Apricot	Burnished Plum
Copper	Golden Coral
Sienna	Indian Earth

Burnt Almond	Bordeaux Wine
Ginger Peachy	

Descriptive terms for PM shades include "mellow," "dusky," "honeyed," "golden," "tawny," "brandied," "amber," "burnt," "shadowed," "slate," "coppery," or "heather." They may have a sheen, as in "copper frost," but they are generally "earthier" than AM shades.

Sunlight (Midday)

Sunlight complexions are characterized by a combination of undertones. If you're in this colortime your best makeup shade is usually a balanced beige with equal amounts of warm and cool undertones. These shades are often called:

Natural Beige	Ivory
Medium Beige	Bisque
Soft Beige	Mocha (for slightly
Basic Beige	darker skin)
	Natural Tan (for slightly
	darker skin)

When in doubt, try a natural beige tone that blends with your skin and add blusher to cheeks, chin, and forehead.

The Midday colors are subtle, muted, and delicious—fresh fruit sherbet shades. Eye shadows are in subtle neutral tones.

Sunlight blushers, rouges, lipsticks, glosses, and nail polishes have names like:

Blushing Peach	Rosewood
Midday Rose	Chestnut
Fresh Melon	Gentle Grape

Since the Midday colors dip into both of the other two palettes, you might also try the subtler shades from both the AM and PM palettes.

Crossover colors in makeup shades may be used by all palettes; such shades as aubergine, raisin, deep wine, and true red often make beautiful basics. If you are wearing red, but don't like red lips, deepen the color with a bit of brown or outline your lips in red and fill in with a softer shade.

Can You Change Your Colortime Cosmetics?

Is it possible to switch from one colortime to another by changing makeup base shades? Yes, but tricky. Since you don't want that line of demarcation where the makeup base ends, it is best to closely match your skin. But if you do want to switch occasionally, blend very carefully at the jawline by using a slightly dampened sea sponge to carry the color down on the neck.

You can change your lipstick and blusher to blend with the base. The really tricky part is changing your natural eye color! Colored contact lenses are one solution (but it's quite expensive). If you have hazel eyes, it's less difficult because these are the chameleon shades that tend to reflect the color you wear nearest your face.

Another obstacle to changing colortimes is hair color. You certainly wouldn't want to change your hair color every other day. Wigs are passé. Scarves and hats are in, but because you don't wear your hat with your nightgown, you eventually have to face the moment of truth.

So you can fool Mother Nature; it's not impossible, but it is difficult. If you keep switching colortimes, however, you'll have to have all the right shades in that particular palette.

Models and actresses must make frequent color changes, but wide-ranging make-up shades are part of the tools of their trade. **Jeff Angell** is an award winning Hollywood makeup artist who works with many of the top models and stars in films and TV. What he does to a face is pure magic! He often changes a model's colortime for cosmetic ads, but the lighting is also changed. Since we can't all walk around (unfortunately) with special lights focused on us at all times, it is most flattering to stay in your own colortime, especially for daytime makeup.

Jeff feels that most women don't experiment enough with makeup. He suggests applying samples of your makeup base, eye colors, lipsticks, and blushers on cardboard (not white paper) to see how a particular group of colors is going to look together. It's a trick that he uses that can help you decide if you like the way they blend and alert you to possible mistakes. He also feels, and I agree with him, that white makeup under the eyes can accentuate circles rather than hide them. Try an off-white or flesh tone instead.

Most women prefer a few dependable eyeshadow colors, a basic makeup and blusher shade, and a few lip colors. Once you have the basics, you can have fun with the extras. And it really is fun to play with new colors. Nothing dates a woman more than an antiquated hairstyle or an outmoded lipstick shade. Fuschia may have been fascinating on her when she was twenty, but time does march on. It is impossible to have a single lipstick shade that "goes with everything."

You may have trouble with "odd" shades that are difficult to find the right lipstick for. Rather than try to match a blue-wine sweater with a lot of brown undertone, for example, buy a shade like Wine and Roses (AM) and blend it with Burnished Brown (PM). Or get out some of your rejects (the ones you can't bring yourself to throw away) and try them with a new color. See how inventive and creative you can be. A word of caution—be careful of intensely purpled or very blue-based lipsticks if your teeth are yellowed. Soften the blue undertone or warm it up slightly.

Hair Color

If you color your hair, choosing the right shade can be more confusing than choosing cosmetics. The name of the color will generally give you a good idea of whether it is AM, Midday, or PM—Arctic Blonde

(AM), Honey Blonde (PM), and Neutral Blonde (Midday), for example. The photo on the box or in an illustrated brochure can be a fairly good indicator of the color inside. Many terms are either not descriptive enough or too difficult to classify by name. "Frivolous Fawn" or "Bashful Beige" might be anybody's guess!

Body chemistry can affect hair just as it does cosmetics. Your hair may have a natural red or gold tone that has a tendency to come through whatever color you use. You may find this an attractive undertone, especially if you have PM coloring. But if you want to play down the red-gold, use a product with either cool or ash undertones.

Conversely, if you have used a product that has given your hair a green or blue-green tinge, a reddish shade can help to neutralize the blue-green. If you are blonde or grey and have used a product that added unwanted violet or silver, a golden shade is a good neutralizer. Strange things can happen to your skin tone if your hair coloring clashes with your colortime. Hair is a crucial part of your self-image, and it's well worth the time it takes to get the color right.

If this seems totally confusing, not to worry. Your local beauty supply store can advise you or your hairdresser can help. If you've really made a mess, let a professional undo the damage. Limit your experiments with new colors to small strands of hair until you are sure of how the color will respond to you.

The following guidelines can help you with hair color choices; the Color Clock can be a tremendous help. Your natural color is never wrong. But if you want to change it, cover it up, or enhance it, use the shades that will appear most natural.

Blondes

Sunrise
If you are an AM blonde, ash or platinum tones will blend best with your skin. A bit of yellow is all right, but brassy gold will not blend with your cool skin. You will want to eliminate as much gold as

possible. The shades that most closely describe Sunrise blondes are:

Ash Blonde	Platinum
Nordic	Cool Beige

Sunset

If you are in the sun a good deal, your hair tends to turn a yellow-gold. As a PM blonde, this can be a blessing because golden undertones will blend with your skin and hair, looking terrific and natural. In choosing hair colors, PM blondes look for key words like:

Warm Blonde	Warm Beige
Golden Blonde	Amber
Honey Blonde	

Sunlight

If you are a Midday blonde, a combination of blonde shades can be very effective. Because you tend to have variety in your natural color and your skin has both warm and cool undertones, variegated hair can be extremely flattering. Streaking or weaving is especially good on Middays; shades from the AM and PM palette may be combined.

Redheads

The term redhead covers a wide range of colors. True auburn tends to flatter AM skins because it has a relatively cool cast compared with the rust-copper undertones of a golden PM red. PM redheads with sallow or yellowed skin should be wary of intensifying golden tones, which may emphasize the sallowness; a mixture of auburn and coppery shades might work better than straight copper for these skin colors.

Red hair may have a tendency to become "brassy." Regardless of your colortime, be careful of harsh tones if your skin is aging or sallow. You may have to switch to a less vivid color to keep the brassiness out.

Sunrise

AM red shades have names like:

Sherry   Medium Auburn
Berry   Dark Auburn
Light Auburn

Sunset

PM red shades are apt to be called:

Coppertone   Red Penny
Sun Bronze   Honey Red
Reddish Blonde   Burnished Copper

Sunlight (Midday)

Midday redheads are never bright. If you're a redheaded Midday, your color is more subtle and often streaked. Combined auburn and copper tones are a good choice. In many instances, natural redheads will go from AM or PM to Midday when their hair begins to streak with grey. The softer shades are more flattering in later years than the bright or deep tones of youth.

Redheads in every colortime must be careful of fiery reds and oranges in clothing because they may compete or clash with their hair and overshadow it. If you're a PM redhead who loves these colors, use them as accents or in prints. Tawny shades like terra cotta, peach, warm browns, bordeaux, terre brun, apricot and raisin are better to use near your hair than brilliant orange-reds. AM auburns, with their cool red tones, look wonderful in shades of raisin, rose-pink coral, cocoa, bittersweet, and terre brun. Midday reds are terrific in melon, orange blossom, mocha, chestnut, raisin, and terre brun.

Browns

Sunrise

AM Browns usually have ash undertones, which may range from quite light to very dark. If a red tone is present, it is auburn or berry colored.

Sunrise brown shades are often described as:

Light Ash Brown	Dark Ash Brown
Medium Ash Brown	Sable

Sunset

PM browns tend to accent the amber tones. Colors in this range (from lightest to darkest undertones) are often called:

Warm Brown	Honeyed Brown
Golden Brown	Russet

Sunlight

Midday browns are variegated combinations of warm and cool tones. The most natural looking combination will combine both the AM and PM colortime shades.

Grey

Once upon a time, all little grey-haired ladies put blue rinses on their hair. Golden tones in grey were a definite no-no. In spite of the trend to more natural greying, most grey hair coloring products continue to boast that they will "get the yellow out" as though it were some sort of dreaded affliction!

If you are PM, let the yellow stay *in*. Nature intended for your hair to blend with your skin and eyes. If your skin is sallow, you may want to liven up the grey somewhat by giving it sheen, which can be done with a good conditioner, or you may want to go to a warm grey rinse. These are more difficult to find than the cool AM shades and their names are often misleading. Some "Snow Whites" and "Pearly Whites" are in the warm range. You will simply have to experiment.

Middays look great with salt and pepper or mixed greys. But no blue tints, please, for Midday or PM. You will look absolutely ill.

A hint of blue in the silvery tones of an AM grey can be striking, but an AM risks looking dated when too much blue is added. Try a good conditioner on your natural color. If this doesn't do it, there are lots of good AM greys on the market, with names like "Silver," "Cool White," and "Silver Diamond." Grey and white hair, like blonde, tends to yellow in sunlight. If you are an AM grey, remember to protect your hair from bright sunlight.

The term "Salt and Pepper" describes those who are changing from their natural darker color to grey. The emerging grey of AM people will show a silvery or pure white tone. A pewter grey mixture is characteristic of PMs and the greying hair of Middays tends to have both warm and cool tones.

Blacks

True blue-black is always AM. This is why tinted blue-black hair can look so phony on some people. They are Midday or PM and it simply does not go with their skin and eyes. This can make tinted black hair painfully obvious—more so than any other color. This is especially true for men, because they lack the cosmetics to help their skin tones blend with the tinted shade.

It is also very difficult to retain blue-black hair in later years because it can be so harsh next to yellowing or aging skin. I always suggest a dark cool brown or a brown mixed with a smidgin of black for "maturing"

AMs, a mixture of medium to dark browns for Middays, and a dark honeyed brown for PMs.

Blue-black really does look best on flawless, fair, or youthful AM skin. The natural hair color of "black"-haired PMs, as dark as it may seem, is really deep brown or umber brown-black rather than blue-black. There is no black in the Sunlight palette.

If your hairstylist does your coloring, please introduce him or her to the Color Clock. Hairstylists can do a fantastic job on color without it, if they have a good eye for color. But because not all hairstylists are colorists, they may be tempted to choose a color simply because it is in their colortime—not yours!

Men and Hair Color

These same general guidelines also apply to men. Although there is still something of a stigma attached to the use of hair coloring by men, acceptance of this practice is growing rapidly.

If you are coloring your hair because of your self-image, if it makes you feel better about yourself, or if greying hair makes you feel older and you don't like the feeling, by all means do it! But please remember that grey or white hair can be very attractive and appealing. Look at **Johnny Carson, Cary Grant, John Forsythe,** and **Merv Griffin.**

If you do color your hair, you must be willing to make the commitment to keep it up regularly. Regrowth of the unwanted color looks obvious and unkempt. A slight "highlighting" or streaking is often better than a solid shade—regrowth is far less obvious and you can go for a longer period of time without recoloring. It is also best for men to stay with subtle colors. Please—no severe blue-blacks after 30. It looks like shoe polish on the head, and the starkness draws attention to less-than-youthful skin.

As we age, our skin picks up lines, wrinkles and yellow pigment, and may become spotty. Hair color should thus be "softer" to deemphasize these changes. Do not try to duplicate the exact shade that you had at age 20. The haircolor that's gorgeous on a 25-year-old can be a disaster at age 50.

For Men Only

When I do color swatches for a male client, I give him many of the same shades that I give my female clients in the same colortime. Many areas of a man's wardrobe give him the chance to experience the fun and creativity that color can bring. Jogging suits, cushy velour tops and robes, sportswear, and emblem knit shirts can be bought in every color of the rainbow.

In spite of having more freedom in dress and clothing colors than ever before, most men still need to dress conservatively for business. So I give them their basic colors, just as I give them to female clients, including the shirting that blends best with their coloring.

I find that the best colors for a man to build a business wardrobe around are the crossover colors. They work for all palettes and there is enough variety to keep a wardrobe from getting dull. You can always spark it up with a shirt in your own palette like a soft mauve, a light lavender, or a deep peach. But you can stay within the framework of the most basic crossover colors and have a very workable, acceptable wardrobe.

The staples, of course, are the Grey Flannel, charcoal, navy, and black, and variations of brown. Wine, aubergine, raisin, evergreen, and true red can be used as accent colors in ties and handerchiefs. Sand, taupe, light grey, sky blue, and yellow make excellent shirting colors, both as solids and in combinations.

The crossovers are also the source of "Power" colors, which you'll find out about in Chapter 4. Since the crossover colors work for all palettes, I usually suggest suit and/or jacket colors on the basis of hair. Grey and navy are excellent with grey, black, blonde, or silver hair, as are variations of brown with brown and red hair. Eyes and skin are often the source of shirt and/or tie color.

O. J. Simpson wears his PM browns and beiges handsomely, as does **Robert Redford,** who favors leather and suedes. And, of course, **Paul Newman** is terrific in his AM blues and grey.

The most common mistakes made in coordinating a wardrobe are:

1. TOO MONOCHROMATIC—Light grey suit, pale blue shirt, pale blue tie.

2. TOO MANY DIRECTIONAL PATTERNS—Plaids, stripes, and patterns, each headed in a different direction.

3. WRONG MOOD—Sporty shirt with business suit.

4. WRONG TEXTURE—Silky tie with heavy wool suit.

5. WRONG COLORS—Too many colors from opposite colortimes.

Among the combinations that will always work when in doubt are:

1. Solid suit, patterned shirt, solid tie

2. Solid suit, patterned tie, solid shirt

3. Solid suit, solid shirt, solid tie—if one element is colorful or contrasting, as with a dark blue suit, off-white shirt, and wine tie.

Other possible combinations for men include:

1. A solid suit with a patterned shirt and patterned tie if one is nondirectional, or soft and quiet. For example: A solid grey suit with a light grey and white pinstripe shirt and a tie in a small paisley print of soft colors, including grey. The tie will always look coordinated when its pattern includes the colors of the suit and/or shirt.

2. A rep tie is acceptable with a striped shirt because it is traditional, your eye is accustomed to this combination, and because diagonal lines are neither vertical nor horizontal. But the colors and textures must blend.

If you do not have a good eye for combinations, or simply want to play it safe, don't put two patterns together. Pick up the colors of the suit or shirt in the tie.

If the suit is in a pattern, such as a glen plaid, it is best worn with a solid shirt and solid tie. For example: A grey glen plaid suit with a light grey shirt and medium grey tie. If the plaid is very muted, a solid shirt with a subtly-patterned tie is possible. A pinstripe suit looks best with a solid shirt and tie, but you could use a tie with a subtle pattern. For example: A navy pinstripe suit with a white shirt and a navy and white tie in a small polka dot. If the pinstripe is hardly discernible, a narrow stripe shirt is possible, but with a solid tie. It is best to wear solids with tweeds to keep from looking too "busy."

Some fashion authorities feel that men's socks should match, blend, or relate to tie color. For example: A red and silver grey striped tie with deep wine socks. Bright red socks would be a bit much—wine is a better choice. They are related to the red in the tie and won't scream at you. Another example would be a sky blue and taupe tie with navy socks. Sky blue is related to navy—and light blue in socks is inappropriate. Light socks give a casual look to an outfit, so they are not right for business or dress wear. I feel that you're always "safe" with the darkest sock colors. If you're not wearing a tie, your socks should match your shoes.

Shirt patterns should be low key and subtle. Against a pale background such colors as brown, wine, grey, dark blue, and even black can work in a patterned shirt but bright colors, such as red, orange, purple, or bright pinks are cheap looking. They can be great for sportswear, but not for a conservative business look.

A touch of brightness sparks a dark tie. Pure white or a dab of color can lift a dark suit, but the area should be small and restricted to the pattern, not the background.

Solids and small patterns are best—small polka dots, narrow stripes, small geometrics, miniature plaids, and subtle paisleys. In general, the fewer the colors, the more formal the tie. A colored or patterned handkerchief in the breast pocket can be added for a touch of color. It should relate to the tie color. Vests can provide a good "pulled together" look. Not only do they disguise a bay window, but when vest and pants match, the body appears taller and slimmer.

Colors vary according to geographical location. Generally, the farther north and east you go, the more conservative the look and the color. Washington, D.C., Boston and environs, and New York (especially in the financial world) are considered among the most conservative. Dark suits and light shirts are the general rule. San Francisco also shares this "eastern" look.

Colors and patterns in suits are lighter and more relaxed in the south and west. Medium-range tans and greys are safe suit colors in these regions. The beige or taupe suit is acceptable in summer in all areas.

If you're a conventional dresser, or work in a conservative industry, black and brown are your best shoe shades. But if you like to experiment, or you're in a "glamour" industry, try the neutral shoe colors, especially in warm climates or weather, or for sportswear. Remember, lighter neutrals work only with lighter colored clothing.

Los Angeles is relaxed and often trendy. The top executives in most industries, however, are often conservatively dressed. Texas and other areas of the Southwest also have their own special look. It is okay for them to wear big 10-gallon Stetsons and pointed boots with business suits, but if you are an outsider and affect that look, you will look just like that—an outsider.

Goof-Proof Combinations

I often suggest that clients who are interested in simplifying their wardrobes start with a two-color (duochromatic) plan. Choose both your main color and the blending second color from the same colortime palette. The most practical choice, and the best way to stretch your budget, is to make that second color a neutral or basic shade. It will also make a good accessory color that works well with many other things in your closet.

Some of the best neutrals are the crossover taupes of greige and sand, and pearl grey and grey flannel; but each colortime palette contains other useful shades of beige, tan, grey, and taupe. Check your colortime palette to see what they are.

The darker crossover shades that work well as accessory colors are aubergine, raisin, wine, navy, terre brun, charcoal, and black. These dependable basics always stay in fashion.

To make your choices easier, possible combinations are illustrated in the color section. The following pages will also help you choose "goof-proof" combinations. For a duochromatic combination, simply use a color from the first column (A) with a color from either of the adjacent columns (B). For example: Midday grape and greige.

For a three color (trichromatic) combination, the most practical choice would be one color from "A," another color from "B," and a third shade from one of the neutral colors listed. For example: PM Coral Dust, Brick Red, and Camel.

When you decorate a room, you may combine colors just as you would when decorating your body. But because a room is much larger, you can use many more variations of the colors you choose. For example, the combination of AM Aqua and Mauve Morn could be expanded to include touches of Bright Turquoise and Amethyst for contrast and variety. The colors could also be combined in a print. The next chapter gives you more specific suggestions on how to handle color in your home or office.

As you will discover later in the book, your personality definitely enters into your choices, so some of the combinations will feel just right to you, and others won't be as comfortable. Use this list as a guide.

Sunrise (AM) *Goof-Proof Combinations*

Column A	Column B		
Ice Blue	Opalescent Teal	Raspberry Glacé	Wine
Windsor Blue	Sapphire	Regal Purple	Greige
Celestial Blue	Amethyst	Fuchsia	Pearl Grey
Sky Blue	Orchid Dawn	Watermelon	Crystal Grey
	Aquamarine	Rose-Pink Coral	Grey Flannel
	Shocking Pink	Sea Pink	Sand
	Raisin	Aubergine	Charcoal
	Bittersweet	Mauve-Taupe	Rose-Beige
			Cocoa
Bright Turquoise	Sapphire	Rose-Pink Coral	Bittersweet
Opalescent Teal	Celestial Blue	Shocking Pink	Navy
	Sea Pink	Shell	Rose-Beige
	Sunlight Yellow	Daffodil	Aqua
	Daybreak Yellow	Aqua	Aquamarine
	White	Black	Charcoal
	Crystal Grey	Pearl Grey	Mauve Taupe
	Terre Brun		

Column A	Column B		
Aqua Aquamarine	Sapphire Misted Rose Raspberry Glacé Sunlight Yellow Mauve Morn Bright Turquoise Terre Brun	Orchid Dawn Sea Pink Rose-Pink Coral Daffodil Opalescent Teal Cocoa Greige	Sand Bittersweet Pearl Grey Crystal Grey Charcoal Navy
Emerald	Misted Rose Raspberry Glacé Sunlight Yellow White Crystal Grey	Shell Daybreak Yellow Sky Blue Black Pearl Grey	Navy Rose-Beige Bittersweet Terre Brun
Seafoam Green	Opalescent Teal Shocking Pink Lavender Frost Greige Rose-beige	Wine Misted Rose Sand Mauve-Taupe Cocoa	Mauve Morn Fuchsia Pearl Grey Crystal Grey
Regal Purple Amethyst	Windsor Blue Sky Blue Greige Bittersweet Cocoa Mauve Morn	Ice Blue Lavender Frost Raisin Terre Brun Mauve Taupe	Grey Flannel Crystal Grey Pearl Grey White Orchid Dawn
Rose-Pink Coral Watermelon	Ice Blue Sky Blue Bright Turquoise Emerald Sunlight Yellow Seafoam Green	Celestial Blue Opalescent Teal Evergreen Rose-Beige Daffodil Navy	White Grey Flannel Crystal Grey Charcoal Pearl Grey Black
Raspberry Glacé	Opalescent Teal Sky Blue White Evergreen Lavender Frost Shell Mauve Morn Pearl Grey	Ice Blue Windsor Blue Emerald Seafoam Green Sea Pink Orchid Dawn Crystal Grey	Black Raisin Navy Cocoa Sand Charcoal Grey Flannel

Column A	Column B		
Lavender Frost	Opalescent Teal	Wine	Terre Brun
	Regal Purple	Amethyst	Bittersweet
	Raisin	Aubergine	Pearl Grey
	Aqua	Raspberry Glacé	Crystal Grey
	Windsor Blue	Greige	Grey Flannel
	Mauve-Taupe	Sand	Charcoal
Evergreen	Sky Blue	Orchid Dawn	Sand
	Rose-Pink Coral	Misted Rose	Bittersweet
	Sea Pink	Shell	Terre Brun
	Daffodil	Daybreak Yellow	Rose-Beige
	Watermelon	Navy	Cocoa
	Mauve Taupe		
Sapphire	Emerald	Windsor Blue	Terre Brun
	Bright Turquoise	Opalescent Teal	Charcoal
	Bittersweet	Black	Greige
	White	Pearl Grey	Sand
	Crystal Grey	Grey Flannel	
Orchid Dawn	Sapphire	Bittersweet	Navy
	Celestial Blue	Ice Blue	Cocoa
	Seafoam	Black	Raisin
	White	Mauve-Taupe	Wine
	Greige	Pearl Grey	Aubergine
	Crystal Grey	Fuchsia	Misted Rose
Daffodil	Ice Blue	Celestial Blue	Terre Brun
	Kelly Green	Windsor Blue	Grey Flannel
	Rose-Pink Coral	Limeade	Crystal Grey
	Evergreen	Bittersweet	Pearl Grey
Cherry	Ice Blue	Sky Blue	Sand
True Red	Black	Navy	Pearl Grey
	White	Charcoal	Crystal Grey
	Grey Flannel	Greige	
Kelly Green	Sunlight Yellow	Daffodil	White
Limeade	Daybreak Yellow	Shell	Charcoal
	Terre Brun	Bittersweet	Grey Flannel
	Sand	Mauve-Taupe	Rose-Beige

Column A	Column B		
Wine Aubergine Raisin	Celestial Blue Sky Blue Misted Rose Mauve Taupe	Windsor Blue Ice Blue Mauve Morn Crystal Grey	Pearl Grey Greige Orchid Dawn Sand
Ruby Shocking Pink Fuchsia	Shell Aquamarine Grey Flannel Ice Blue Navy	Misted Rose White Rose-Beige Sky Blue Pearl Grey	Aqua Bittersweet Evergreen Black Crystal Grey

Sunlight (Midday) *Goof-Proof Combinations*

Column A	Column B		
Peach Melba Melon	Evergreen Creme De Menthe Mauve Mushroom Dove Grey Flannel Wedgwood Limoges	Teal Green Mint Vanilla Terre Brun Pearl Grey Jade Delft	Mocha Terre Brun China Blue Orange Blossom Soft Turquoise Lilac Chestnut
Dusty Rose Strawberry Cream	Evergreen Soft Turquoise Sky Blue Mauve Raisin Limoges Grape Wine	Plum Cordial China Blue Teal Green Jade Rosewood Wedgwood Mint	Mocha Sand Dove Pearl Grey Creme Caramel Greige Aubergine
Raisin Aubergine Wine	Strawberry Cream Mauve Orchid Wedgwood Greige	Dusty Rose China Blue Limoges Lilac Sand	Mushroom Dove Pearl Grey Sky Blue

Sunlight (Midday) *Con't*

Column A	Column B		
Chestnut Creme Caramel	Vanilla China Blue Melon Bisque Orchid Delft Black	Teal Green Peach Melba Mauve Wisteria Orange Blossom Terre Brun Pearl Grey	Dove Grey Flannel Sand Navy Grape Dusty Rose
Banana Buttercream Lemonade	Mint Creme de Menthe Orange Blossom Celadon Soft Turquoise Greige	China Blue Melon Chestnut Limoges Dove	Delft Sky Blue Navy Pearl Grey Grey Flannel
Creme de Menthe	Strawberry Cream Dusty Rose Melon Mocha Bark Lemonade	Raspberry Sherbet Banana Peach Melba Mauve Bisque	Sunlight Yellow Dove Pearl Grey Grey Flannel Greige
Jade	Teal Green Strawberry Cream Bark Bisque China Blue	Dusty Rose Melon Raspberry Sherbet Greige Pearl Grey	Sage Orchid Navy Dove Mushroom
China Blue Sky Blue	Grape Wine Banana Plum Cordial Mauve Orchid Creme Caramel Bisque Greige	Mocha Mauve Raspberry Sherbet Sage Dusty Rose Sunlight Yellow Peach Melba Terre Brun	Dove Pearl Grey Grey Flannel Aubergine Raisin Wine Sand Mushroom

Sunlight (Midday) *Con't*

Column A	Column B		
Wedgwood	Orchid	Lemonade	Pearl Grey
	Orange Blossom	Lilac	Dove
	Wisteria	Melon	Grey Flannel
	Plum Cordial	Mocha	Aubergine
	Raspberry Sherbet	Banana	Wine
	Grape	Chestnut	Black
	Mushroom	Raisin	Greige
	Bark	Vanilla	Terre Brun
Limoges	Celadon	Buttercream	Plum Cordial
	Melon	Sage	Creme Caramel
	Orange Blossom	Banana	Dusty Rose
	Sunlight Yellow	Rosewood	Strawberry Cream
	Orchid	Peach Melba	Dove
	Grape	Bisque	Pearl Grey
	Greige	Mocha	Grey Flannel
	Bark	Raspberry Sherbet	Terre Brun
Grape	Mauve	China Blue	Chestnut
Wisteria	Vanilla	Lilac	Sand
	Orchid	Wedgwood	Greige
	Dusty Rose	Buttercream	Dove
	Creme Caramel	Raisin	Pearl Grey
	Grey Flannel	Rosewood	Mushroom
Sage	Wine	Dusty Rose	Sky Blue
	Mauve	Strawberry Cream	China Blue
	Peach Melba	Vanilla	Navy
	True Red	Bark	Grape
Evergreen	Strawberry Cream	Mauve	Dusty Rose
	Peach Melba	Sand	Celadon
	Melon	Navy	Bisque
	Greige	Banana	Dove
	Creme Caramel	Raspberry Sherbet	

Sunset (PM) *Goof-Proof Combinations*

Column A	Column B		
Brick Red Tomato Red	Khaki Sunlight Yellow Navy Terre Brun Honey Greige Cinnamon	Autumn Gold Curry Cream Black Purple Heather Avocado	Bay Leaf Camel Warm Taupe Smoke Grey Flannel Bronze
Paprika Geranium	Terra Cotta Cream Apricot Harvest Gold Coral Dust Sky Blue Dusk Blue Hunter	Dusk Blue Peach Peacock Horizon Purple Deep Periwinkle Cadet Blue Khaki Black	Camel Charcoal Smoke Greige Navy Honey Avocado Grey Flannel
Curry Honey	Burnt Orange Avocado Brick Cream Dill Paprika Deep Teal	Hunter Khaki Terre Brun Sky Blue Bay Leaf Geranium Bordeaux	Deep Periwinkle Hunter Evergreen Smoke Grey Flannel Black Tomato
Magenta Haze	Horizon Purple Lilac Dusk Camel Cadet Blue Dusk Blue Aubergine	Purple Heather Peacock Deep Periwinkle Sky Blue Navy Raisin	Greige Smoke Pearl Grey Grey Flannel Charcoal Wine
Horizon Purple Purple Heather	Cadet Blue Greige Magenta Haze Terre Brun Grey Flannel	Lilac Dusk Cream Raisin Dusk Blue Pearl Grey	Sand Brick Red Deep Periwinkle Smoke

Sunset (PM) *Con't*

Column A	Column B		
Coral Dust	Cadet Blue	Sky Blue	Khaki
	Sunlight Yellow	Dusk Blue	Avocado
	Deep Teal	Peacock	Evergreen
	Hunter	Bay Leaf	Camel
	Deep Periwinkle	Evergreen	Cinnamon
	Lilac Dusk	Peach	Terre Brun
	Brick Red	Terra Cotta	Antique Turquoise
	Charcoal	Smoke	Grey Flannel
Bordeaux	Deep Teal	Dill	Deep Periwinkle
	Khaki	Camel	Sky Blue
	Cadet Blue	Dusk Blue	Coral Dust
	Peacock	Cream	Smoke
	Greige	Warm Taupe	Pearl Grey
	Ash Rose	Lilac Dusk	
Bronze	Curry	Harvest Gold	Smoke
	Navy	Black	Honey
	Charcoal	Cream	
Aubergine	Ash Rose	Dusk Blue	Smoke
Wine	Cadet Blue	Sky Blue	Magenta Haze
Raisin	Peacock	Camel	Lilac Dusk
	Greige	Warm Taupe	Sand
	Deep Periwinkle	Pearl Grey	
Deep Teal	Cinnamon	Terra Cotta	Apricot
	Cadet Blue	Dusk Blue	Peach
	Sand	Greige	Ash Rose
	Cream	Magenta Haze	Greige
	Lilac Dusk	Coral Dust	Smoke
	Navy		
True Red	Black	Charcoal	Cream
	Navy	Smoke	Camel
	Pearl Grey	Khaki	Greige
	Sand		

Sunset (PM) Con't

Column A	Column B		
Antique Turquoise	Cinnamon	Terra Cotta	Honey
	Sand	Peacock	Cream
	Navy	Greige	Grey Flannel
	Warm Taupe	Curry	Charcoal
	Smoke	Black	
Hunter	Ash Rose	Coral Dust	Harvest Gold
Evergreen	Warm Taupe	Greige	Curry
Dill	Honey	Apricot	Sunlight Yellow
	Peach	Paprika	Smoke
	Cinnamon	Camel	Khaki
	Cream	Brick Red	Geranium
Bay Leaf	Terra Cotta	Apricot	Sunlight Yellow
	Coral Dust	Harvest Gold	Brick Red
	Warm Taupe	Greige	Tomato
	Sand	Khaki	Burnt Orange
	Avocado	Bronze	
Burnt Orange	Apricot	Peach	Terre Brun
	Sunlight Yellow	Harvest Gold	Bay Leaf
	Honey	Terra Cotta	Avocado
	Paprika	Navy	Khaki
	Charcoal	Smoke	Sand
	Cream	Camel	

I encourage my clients to play with their color combinations, just as a child does with a box of crayons. You might come up with combinations that are not listed. You can open yourself up to a whole new creative experience. Don't be concerned about how someone else might do it—choose your colortime and let your colors be an expression of you.

Keep an open mind to the excitement of new and interesting color combinations in your chosen colortime and see how you can come alive with color!

To my male readers: It might be difficult for you to relate to colors with "feminine" names like Shocking Pink or Misted Rose. Just think of those vivid preppie cotton knit "alligator" shirts or button down oxford shirts in cotton candy colors and you'll get the picture. Forget the names—just use your palette as your guide.

After all, women have been using so-called masculine colors like hunter green, cadet blue, and navy for years, and it doesn't make us any less ladylike!

Chapter 3

Using Color
With Flair
All Around You

Decorating With Color and Flair

From earliest times, people have chosen to decorate their environments with color. Baskets, pots, textiles, the simplest tools, even the walls of primitive dwellings were embellished with colorful designs. It's possible that the earliest cave dwellers also competed to have the nicest cave on the block! People have always been fascinated with color and used it as part of their surroundings.

Skillful set and interior designers understand the enormous effect of color. The initial impact that a room has on you is that your senses are flooded with color. You will often leave that room remembering color above all else. Your home, no matter how large or small, can be transformed into something wonderful and comfortable through the creative use of color.

Analyze any successful room and you will notice one dominant color or family of colors. Several shades of the same color can pull together furniture from different periods. If you are the eclectic personality who enjoys mixing periods and styles, color can make it all cohesive. As I noted in previous chapters, the most successful color schemes use the color wheel and the Color Clock for combinations as well as inspiration. Both of those circles will keep you from running around in circles, trying to make color choices.

Most people share their environments with others. If you have a roommate, husband, wife, or children living under your roof, have them take the Colortime Quiz. If they're all attracted to the same colortime, you simply decorate in those colors and everybody is happy.

But what happens if two or more people who live under one roof prefer different colortimes for decorating? Who wins out? Sometimes the person with the strongest personality does. Men will often defer to women when it comes to decorating because it has traditionally been a woman's role. But traditional roles are changing rapidly and men should have their say in color choices. It is their environment, too, and they should be comfortable with the choices.

Chances are that palette preferences will vary within a family, but there are several solutions. If each person has his or her own bedroom, obviously that room could be done in the occupant's preferred colortime. When rooms are shared, such as bedrooms or mutual living areas, the people involved have to reach a compromise.

When two people live together and one is drawn to Sunrise colors and the other to Sunset, they may wind up fighting tooth and nail over every lampshade and toothbrush holder. I have been called in to mediate several such locked-horn situations. I find that the happiest solution for people from these opposite colortime palettes is to compromise with lighter and deeper values of the Sunlight colortime, since that palette overlaps into both of the others.

Because the Sunlight palette does not contain the vivid colorings of Sunrise or Sunset, it is the palette least apt to offend. If you are a Sunrise compromising with a Sunset, and each of you feels the need for a splash of brilliance somewhere, use the guideline of dominance and subordination and you'll both be happy. Do the room (or house) in a dominant Sunlight color and pull in a subordinate bright touch from either the Sunrise or Sunset palette.

Another effective, perhaps more pleasing compromise is to use cross-over colors in combinations. Since crossovers are part of every colortime, most people can relate to them and feel comfortable with them. For example: Wine, or aubergine, or raisin and grey might be used with a touch of sky blue. Or navy and taupe could be combined with accents of true red. Evergreen and sky blue might be brightened by a hint of sunlight yellow.

Monochromatic neutrals can also be effective compromises for people in differing colortimes. Do remember to use a variety of textures and surfaces or these neutrals can become very monotonous.

Rooms That Flow

Rooms other than bedrooms can also be done in the colortime of the person who spends the most time in that room. If you spend a lot of time in the kitchen and love to cook, you really should surround yourself with the colortime that pleases you the most. If cooking is more of a chore than a pleasure, you might be even more eager to surround yourself with a pleasing colortime palette.

If the man of the house loves to watch TV and relax in the family room, he is entitled to be surrounded by the colors he likes best. I firmly believe that children should be allowed to participate in color choices for their rooms, as long as they are not ridiculously bizarre. If your teenager requests punk rock purple and neon green, you might have trouble with your reaction, but their rooms are their private domains and, to use a cliche, we all need our own "space," as well as our own colors.

Bedrooms are rarely visible from the living room area, especially if the doors are kept closed, so you really don't have to be concerned about the color scheme used in the rest of the house. You're not likely to use the same colors in a baby's room that you use in your own bedroom, so you can give everyone his or her favorite colors in the bedrooms. If a den is not visible from the living area, it may be done in a different colortime than the rest. Think of the people who are going to use each room, and of the mood you are trying to convey in that space.

If, however, you have an open floor plan and many rooms are visible from a central point, or you live in a small home or apartment, you do want to keep a thread of colortime continuity winding through your rooms. Your eye will find a natural pathway, and the rooms will flow one into the other, creating the illusion of more space. The same is true of adjacent rooms where one room is visible from the next, such as a kitchen that adjoins a family room, bedrooms and adjoining baths, entryways, and living rooms.

In open floor plans, or in small apartments or townhouses, the ideal solution is to connect your rooms without handling your color combinations in exactly the same way. Reverse your colortime schemes as you progress from one area to another. For example, if your living room was done in an AM combination of dominant emerald, with mauve morn as the secondary color, the color scheme could be reversed in the adjoining dining room area to make mauve morn dominant and emerald subordinate.

Increasing Color Confidence

Beware of the spouse or roommate who tells you to go ahead and decorate in whatever color you like. The day the first piece of furniture arrives, you may hear something like "Why in the world did you choose *that* color?" I have heard many women say, "My husband couldn't care less what colors I use." Unless he is color blind (which is in fact a possibility), he will have some sensitivity to color.

Have him look at the three pages of colortime palettes and ask him to name his favorite. If he still says he couldn't care less, take him to an eye doctor and go ahead and make your own choices. He can't complain later that you didn't ask his opinion.

What about the neighbor or friend who comes into the house and says, after looking at the new chair you just bought, "Do you really like that color?" If the color is "new" and quite different from your usual safe choices, and your confidence is a little shaky to begin with, you can be demolished by a comment like that.

Don't let such remarks throw you. If you have used your preference quiz as a guide and shopped with your color swatches so that you're not relying on memory alone, you can be confident enough to rely on your own judgement.

Just remember that people's opinions tend to be based on their own color preferences. Have you ever shopped with a friend, considered something in a color that you really weren't sure of and heard the friend say, "Oh, **I** love that color; **you** have to have it!" That is exactly what he or she means—they love that color and it's probably in their favorite colortime.

I wouldn't want to break up a beautiful friendship, but it is difficult for most people to be really objective about color unless they are trained professionals with enough experience to be truly objective. Most people can't help but respond to color on a subjective level. Chances are that if you take your friend's advice, when you get the color home you'll never really feel comfortable with it.

You are better off following your own instinct and reinforcing that instinct with your colortime swatches. That way you won't end up with an expensive mistake. If you do shop with another person, try someone with a really objective eye, or someone else in your colortime!

After you've gotten feedback from family and/or roommates and decided on a colortime in a particular setting, where do you go from there? The next step in decorating is to choose your main color from within that colortime. If you must decorate around existing colors, such as a carpet that has to stay, then you must obviously consider that carpet color in terms of your scheme and move on from there.

In getting your color picture together, start with:

1. the major or dominant area of walls and floor, then move on to colors for:

2. the secondary area of window treatments and larger upholstered pieces. Last come

3. the accent pieces of pillows, occasional chairs, and other accessories.

Perhaps you have favorite objects—dishes in the china cabinet in a wedgwood blue—that will inspire a color scheme. Or perhaps you have found a chair in a printed fabric that includes all of your colortime harmonies. All you have to do is expand on those harmonies to complete the room.

Sources of Inspiration

There are at least twenty wonderful directions to take in your search for ideas on developing a color scheme.

Sunrise (AM)

Sparkling crystals
The sophistication of mirrors, glass, polished chromes; the starkness of black and white with one strong accent.

Clean, clear water colors

If you love the ocean blues and blue-greens, seafoam green, cool neutrals, and the white-caps of the waves, this is a good place to start. Although they are traditional for bedrooms because of their serenity, these AM colors will work in a living room.

Gemstones

Exciting brilliants in sparkling tones of sapphires, rubies, or emeralds.

The dawning of a new day

Cool greys, bright reds, and a flash of a vivid daybreak yellow.

Pure primaries, paintbox and jelly bean colors

Exciting brilliants, active, whimsical, and childlike. Unsophisticated and good for playrooms and children.

Sunlight (Midday)

A field of fresh spring flowers

The whitewashed brilliance of a meadow in full sunlight. Lilacs, wisteria, orange blossoms, and mint.

Delicious tints and shadings

Fruits and berries, ice cream, sherbet and confection colors. Plum cordials, peach melbas, and buttercream.

Desert sands

Soft and sun-bleached beiges and taupes with muted accents of sage, rosewood, or celadon.

Mother of pearl, seashells, and sand

Iridescent mauves, light peaches and greys, taupes and soft whites, soft turquoise, Limoges blue.

Sunset (PM)

Country and mountain
Warm burnished woods, hearth, home, herbs, heather, and home-baked bread. Hunter greens, warm browns, harvest gold, honey, cream whites.

Dusk
Mellowed, dusky blues, greyed purples, teal, periwinkle, and grey-greens of a sky at nightfall.

Sunset and Fire
The deep warmth of fiery shades of burnt orange, warm, intense geranium reds, horizon purples, and magenta haze.

Exotic and Spicy
Paprika, cinnamon, dill, and curry in paisleys mixed with bronze.

Southwestern American Indian
Terra cotta , clay, Navajo red, and antique turquoise set against silver.

All Colortimes
These could be in any of the appropriate blending colortimes. I'm sure you can think of more. All you have to do is keep your eyes, and your mind, open.

The great outdoors—If you are an outdoor person and love nature scenes, crossover evergreen and lush plants can provide a fresh, tranquil background. Floral patterns from any colortime will blend with versatile evergreen.

Favorite objects—Ruby glass, shells, an antique coffee mill surrounded by the appropriate colortime.

Travel mementos—Wall hangings, a throw rug, leaves from a New England autumn.

A piece of sculpture, a painting, or a poster—Use the colors of a piece of artwork you already own, or take a trip to a museum for inspiration.

A decorating book or magazine.

A room setting in the home furnishings department of a department store or decorator's shop.

A beautiful wall covering, a bedspread, a scarf, or piece of clothing in a striking pattern that catches your eye can inspire a color scheme.

Eliminating Expensive Mistakes

When you have decided on the colortime you will use, and the dominant color from that colortime, you are then ready to use the color wheel to decide which combination to use—monochromatic, duochromatic, etc. The best advice I can give you is to work with color swatches for every single thing you do. This is the most efficient way to check the harmony of your color scheme.

The size of the swatches should relate to the way the colors will be used in the actual room. Make your dominant color the large swatch, the subordinate color a little more than half that size, and your accent colors a scant one-fourth of the largest swatch.

Put them all against a white poster board. Use double-sided cellophane tape for easy removal in case you change your mind. It's so much easier to work this way than with bits of tattered wallpaper and unraveling fabric pinned to paint chips!

It's important to remember that bright colors appear even more so in large doses. The paint chip in the store will look very different when it's on all four walls. I always suggest to clients that they invest in a can of paint, do a section of one wall and let it dry thoroughly (preferably overnight) in order to really judge the color. A cool blue in a small chip might turn icy cold on a wall.

It is really worth the time and effort it takes to gather good-sized samples of possible colors and patterns to see how they blend, particularly in the light of the room they're to be used in. A client I met recently told me that prior to my working with her, she had done her den in a red and navy colonial combination. She ordered her red and navy houndstooth sofa from a small swatch. The day they delivered her expensive new sofa, she almost suffered cardiac arrest. It was a lovely shade of purple. Red and blue do mix at a distance. Colors tend to merge even when you're just a few feet away.

Purple can be used as a touch with its red and blue neighbors on the color wheel, but not in an area as large as the sofa. She wanted a duo-chromatic combination, and wound up with a trichromatic divided almost equally between red, navy, and purple. She eventually had it re-upholstered because it was so obtrusive in the room. It was an expensive mistake that never would have happened if she had gotten a large swatch and viewed it from a distance next to the other colors.

Climbing The Wrong-Colored Walls

The colors of the walls and ceiling (including windows and doors) are critical to the success of any room. They are the background that sets the stage for the room's atmosphere, and often account for more than two thirds of the available space. Your biggest wall-treatment decision will be: Do you want the walls to remain in the background, or do you want them to be a major element of the decor? Generally the more colorful the other furnishings are, the less color you need in the walls.

A good example of walls as neutral backgrounds is used in one of the most incredibly imaginative homes I have ever seen. Designer **Tony Duquette,** who has done, among other things, award-winning theatre sets and a castle in Ireland, and his artist wife Elizabeth live in a studio that was once a theatre on a modest street in the heart of Hollywood. You would never guess from the outside what treasures lie within!

Old Spanish doors open to an "Arabian Nights" PM setting of glittering gold and crystal, with complementary tones of greens and reds in the oriental carpets and plush velvet sofas and chairs. I have been in their home twice, for very special parties, and I left each time feeling as though I had visited a fantasy land.

Although he has a penchant for opulence, one of the nicest things about this charming man is his ability to work with the simplest objects of nature, such as shells, stones, coral, and even fish bones. He told me once that beauty, not luxury, is what he values most, and that you can find beauty in the simplest and often most unexpected places.

Business manager **David Flynn** and his wife, actress **Jane Seymour**, live in a house in the Hollywood Hills that *Vogue* refers to as "light-filled." It is, to be more exact, "sunlight-palette filled."

This beautiful airy house is done in a background of eggshell and light beiges in walls and sofas. Touches of luscious pastels are sprinkled against the neutral backdrop—misty greyed-green, lilac, and pale melon.

The dining room is done in light peach and blue with terra cotta tile; natural wood tones are used throughout. Baby Katherine's room is a Sunrise colortime fantasy of what a little girl's room might look like. It's done with white wicker furniture and white eyelet on the trundle bed. Lollipop reds, yellows, blues, and pinks are used as accents and her lamp is a white duck with a cheerful yellow bill that lights up!

Paintings and other art are often displayed against neutral backgrounds to avoid color "wars." **Andy Williams** uses neutral walls as a background for his collection of contemporary paintings, Navajo rugs, and pueblo jars. *Architectural Digest* describes Andy as having a "gift of warmth" which is translated into his Sunset-colored environment. He prefers paintings of sunflowers to what he calls "windswept, dreary, cold, wintry pictures."

Andy indicated to me his love of warm colors. He likes the hot corals, honey beiges, and avocados of the PM palette. If he were planting a rose garden, he would choose burnished orange-yellow talisman roses.

Your paint brush can become a magic wand. A fresh coat of paint can make an instant transformation and give a clean, new look. If you are stretching your budget, it is the least expensive way to redecorate. The more coats of paint you use, the truer the color will be. Yellows and pastel pinks often need three coats; two coats will do for most other colors. Remember that color intensifies and becomes darker than the paint chip when applied to the wall.

Use your colortime swatches in order to make a pleasing choice for your walls. If the color of this dominant influence doesn't blend with the other colors in the palette you've chosen, you'll feel like climbing the walls rather than living with them!

Uncommon Solutions for Common Problems

Painted surfaces can work magic through optical illusion. Walls may be moved without benefit of bulldozers. You may raise the roof or shrink a sofa. Nooks and crannies may mysteriously disappear, or reappear to house an interesting object.

It is best to use a light background in a small room and to keep the window treatment light and airy so that the area is not too cut up. However, a small, dark space like a hallway, entry, alcove, or powder room can be dramatized by doing just the opposite and making the color intense or sparkly. Colors that would be overwhelming in rooms in which you spend a great deal of time can be energizing in small doses.

Deep or vivid shades are most effective in a passageway when it leads to a large, light area—the effect is that of a light at the end of a tunnel.

If you want to lengthen a short hallway or passage, paint the walls a deep tone and keep the floor and ceiling light. Place pictures along the wall in frames to match the ceiling or floor color. This forms a horizontal pattern that the eye will follow to create more length.

In order to open up a cramped space, lighten the hue on the wall you want to expand. For example, if a sofa must be placed on a short wall, lighten both the wall behind it and the wall immediately opposite. The two remaining walls may be darkened to a medium or deeper tone. The same technique works for a narrow room. Paint the narrow walls lighter than the wider wall.

To make a square room less box-like, do one wall in a deeper tone than the other three walls. Dark or warm wall colors enclose a room, light or cool colors open it up. The same principle can be applied to any colortime, since each palette contains both warm and cool colors.

Monochromatic and neutral schemes unify the space in a small room and give it the illusion of greater size. A ceiling will appear higher if it is painted white or a shade lighter than the walls—white or pale colors also give the best light reflection. Simply add white to your wall color and use it on the ceiling. If you opt for white, use the white that blends best with your colortime scheme.

If you want to lower the ceiling, paint it one tone deeper than the walls. Painting a wide band of the ceiling color around the top part of the walls will also give the illusion of a lower ceiling.

To enlarge small windows, use the same shadings as the walls in your window treatment. Mini-blinds and shutters all have built-in vertical or horizontal lines and are excellent expanders. Don't use anything heavy on small windows and allow as much light to come in as possible.

In smaller rooms, it is best to keep the woodwork the same color as the walls. Contrasting colors will break the wall into sections. In larger rooms, woodwork can be used as an interesting contrast, especially if it is embellished, and it can become a charming focal point. In a dull entry or hallway, brightly colored doors can add some cheer.

If an area seems too cluttered with jutting protrusions, such as alcoves, dormers, bookcases, or window seats, do both walls and protrusions in a unifying color. You can turn jigs and jags into interesting room features. A dark alcove, for instance, can be transformed into a dramatic background for some special object or personal treasure—especially if the background is done in a contrasting color.

Who says pipes can't be beautiful? Ask any plumber. Pipes, plumbing, and duct work can be turned into eye catchers, instead of eyesores. Instead of fighting them, make them focal points.

At the **Erving Paper Mills** in Erving, Massachusetts, **Richard Provost,** Corporate Director of Graphics, and Art Director **Sandra Misium** did a marvelous job of coordinating the industrial features of their art department into a very attractive work environment. In a letter to me, they said, "Our goal in developing this department was to create an ambiance of warmth and ease, while stimulating creativity and, thus, productivity. Cognizant of the role of color, particularly in the work environment, we made a conscious decision to employ this vital tool in our effort.

"Our final selection included a pink coral tone, complemented by soft orange, dusty blue, buff, and egg shell. The above-mentioned colors enhanced the interior design, which included reclamation of the natural brick walls, utilization of rich wood panels and cedar beams, and the promotion of an aerial quality (through the enhancement of the existing pipework).

"We believe we achieved our goal for this department. In fact, we think we created an outstanding work environment, the success of which is measured in the declining degree of tension and stress exhibited by our artists."

I admire them for their efforts. By focusing on the softer values of the Midday palette and warm neutral wood tones, they have effected a good compromise for many people working under the same roof.

Many other companies are developing an awareness of the importance of a pleasing work environment. So much of your time is spent on the job—why not make your surroundings as attractive as possible?

Wallcoverings can also give instant color and a marvelous ambiance to a room. Whatever the mood you want to convey—cozy, whimsical, formal, informal, glamorous—there are wallcoverings to express it. Flaws can be concealed and you often get more character with a wall-covering than with a painted surface.

Another big advantage, if you are a do-it-yourselfer, is that even a novice can hang paper. If you are not good at matching patterns or cutting a straight line, leave it to the experts because a botched-up job can really look bad.

Annette Losin, of Woodland Hills, California, designs beautiful effects in wallcovering by using the Color Clock as her guide. She creates border treatments in coordinating colortimes and gets interesting details around windows and doors, outlining beams, kitchen cabinets, and range hoods.

She cleverly covered an outmoded rusted chrome frame on a medicine cabinet in a client's bathroom by using a strip of the striped wallpaper we used on the walls. Instead of replacing a whole custom cabinet, for literally pennies she had a new, terrific-looking treatment, and the rusted chrome disappeared.

Striped papers with contrasting values can create height or width in a room. Color placed effectively in a design can also create a rhythmic flow to draw the eye vertically or horizontally and increase the illusion of room size. Large designs and deep, dark colors make a room appear smaller. Light solid colors and small designs make a room look larger. Many wallcoverings come with companion fabrics so that windows and walls can be coordinated for a more spacious look. The fabrics may also be used in upholstered pieces to unify the room's design.

Foil and mylar papers can brighten as they add depth and interest. They can also visually increase size because of their mirror-like effect. Natural wallcoverings such as burlap, jute, grasscloth, and cork will work with any colortime palette because they are neutral, but because of their warmth are more often used in Midday and PM palettes, especially in studies, offices, and entryways.

Avoid trendy color combinations in wallpapers or any pattern for interiors, especially in equal proportions of the opposite colortimes of AM and PM. Do you remember Sunset golden orange and Sunrise shocking blue-pink? That kind of look gets old very quickly. Whenever possible, start with the wallcovering color and pattern first, and then choose your ceiling and trim colors to blend.

It is also important to choose carpeting that coordinates well with the colors in the colortime you have selected, because it occupies so much space and helps to set the mood of a room. Be sure to check a large carpet sample in daylight (the smallest it should be is 6 inches square) as well as under the artificial lighting of the room setting, since the texture and color are also affected by lighting. Multicolor carpeting can set the colortime of a room and you can draw wonderful shadings from oriental and area rugs to integrate into your rooms.

Tips on Texture

Color can be greatly affected and altered by texture because of light absorption and light reflection. A newly vacuumed soft pile carpet is a good example of this. Shiny surfaces intensify color. Rough weaves deepen color. The same color appears brighter in polished cotton than it does in rough wool.

Matte or flat surfaces absorb light and appear somewhat darker than glossy, light-reflecting surfaces. Colors appear lighter and more lustrous on smooth surfaces that have a sheen. Apricot on a satin pillow will seem much brighter than the apricot cotton loveseat it sits on.

If, for an accent color, you are going to dip into a different colortime than the dominant palette you are using, choose a nappy or shiny changeable texture and the shade will blend better than it would in a dull texture. The changeability of the texture will also give variety to the color and make it more versatile and less apt to offend the eye. For that reason, lustrous silks and synthetics, velvets, velours, velveteens, and polished cottons span the color clock more easily than flat, non-reflective surfaces do.

Patterned For Success

Gone are the days of never combining patterns in the same room, but there are still a few guidelines to consider.

1. If patterns are not similar, such as a flamestitched needlepoint pillow on a floral chair, but contain the same colors, they will work together. Color is the common thread that links them to each other.

2. Similar patterns will also work, but are more interesting if the scale is different. For example, a large plaid den

sofa done in PM dusk blue could be used with a small houndstooth-checked chair done in the same colors.

3. Patterns appear "heavier" than plain fabrics.

4. Remember that the colors of small-patterned fabrics and tweeds tend to blend. A pink and yellow sprig of flowers seen from up close can turn into peach just a few feet away.

Wood paneling, flooring, and furniture can add more pattern to a room but, just as with the other crossover colors in nature, the blues of the sky and the greens of plants, natural wood finishes do not intrude into an environment. Brown is the color of bark and stems and twigs. The eye is accustomed to the many browns that surround us, so a variety of wood tones will harmonize and wood becomes a neutral. The polished surfaces and grains also show undertones that blend with all of the colortimes.

Metallic finishes combine best with specific colortimes. Sunrise colors work best with high gloss, cool tones of silver, chrome, and platinum. Burnished coppers, antiqued golds, bronze, pewter, and antiqued silver work best with the mellow Sunset colors. Brass and gold are metallic versions of crossover sunlight yellow and blend with all palettes. The Sunlight palette combines best with low luster surfaces.

Shiny surfaces often pick up and reflect surrounding colors. For example, a glass and chrome table that usually works best with the AM palette will pick up and reflect the very warm tones of a PM brick red carpeting. Metals are more versatile than painted surfaces because of their reflective quality. Always think in terms of how the colors surrounding metal finishes will affect the color of the metal.

Some antiqued or matte-finished metals reflect very little, if any, of their surroundings. Deep coppers will pick up very little of the coldest AM blues and purples. As a matter of fact, using the principle of complementary color, cool blue colors will intensify copper because they are opposites on the color wheel.

Alleviating Bedroom Boredom

The bedroom is often the last room in the house to be done because it's a fairly private place that others don't usually see. Our bedroom is the closest link to our backyard pool, so there are often hordes of teenagers traipsing through.

Sometimes the bedroom gets so loaded with magazines and books, and closets so crammed with everything imaginable, that the thought of making more of a mess with paint or wallpaper simply overwhelms you.

Think of it as a challenge. How well-organized and terrific you will feel when you empty the closets, throw all the mess away, and find things buried in bureau drawers that you haven't seen in years. You may even find your nightstand under that pile of books in the corner!

If you're not the messy type, but your bedroom has simply gotten boring and needs a little excitement, change the colors. If you want to stay within the same AM colortime that you used before, simply switch from the traditional tranquilizing blues to more romantic sparkling wine and rose-pinks.

Wine and roses are often associated with romance. **Erik Estrada** answered a color word association quiz by placing "candlelight and romance" next to "wine." Yellow means "smiles" to Erik, so sparkling daybreak yellow is used in and around his pool house (where he keeps his motorcycle). A number of other touches from his AM palette appear in his sleek contemporary house, which features lots of bleached wood and black. Two of his favorites in clothing—black and white—are a dramatic complement to his blue-black hair and gleaming white teeth.

To Erik, soft pink is nice, but shocking pink is sexy. Lavender speaks of love, purple shouts it out, and true red spells passion.

The Importance of Lighting

Just as in set design, the right lighting can set the stage to make a home more appealing and attractive. Since lighting affects your perception of color, you should always check prospective colors in both natural and artificial light in the room where the colors will be used.

Daylight from an eastern exposure will intensify a color slightly. When it comes from the south or west, it will redden a color slightly. Northern daylight is the most neutral, and the best light for applying makeup.

There are two kinds of artificial lighting in general use. The most common is incandescent, the bulb that's readily available in any supermarket or drugstore. Incandescent light does not radically change colors, but it does deaden them somewhat. A slightly ambered glow emanates from incandescent lighting, so that warm colors are enhanced and cool colors played down slightly.

Tinted incandescent bulbs are available. If you want to create a special mood, the general guideline is that each color accents similar colors and subdues complementary colors. Aqua, green, and blue bulbs emphasize cool colors; yellow and pink create a warm aura that intensifies warm colors. If you are using a predominantly cool AM palette or the cooler tones of Midday or PM, you may want to experiment with cool-tinted bulbs to see if you like the effect.

Tinted bulbs can add atmosphere to rooms done in neutral color schemes. They can also add drama in a spotlight aimed at a focal point, such as a small art object or even a simple vase.

Fluorescent lights produce three to five times as much light as incandescents and are available in many varieties, ranging froom cool to warm undertones. Soft white floureseants blend best with incandescents for use in the home—particularly the deluxe warm white. Cool white is generally used in workshops, garages, and industrial plants. If you use fluorescents in the kitchen, the deluxe cool white gives the most accurate color, but it's best used with the cool colors in each palette.

The coolly-lit AM marble entryway of songwriter-poet **Rod McKuen's** home is elegantly perfect. But my favorite accent in this lovely home sits on the coffee table in the large living room. It is Rod's trademark—a pair of over-sized colorful ceramic sneakers!

Chapter 4

Using Color To Influence Others

Yang or Yin?

Color is a very effective form of communication. We say a lot about ourselves through the colors we use. Circle the words below that you feel reflect your personality.

Extrovert	Introvert
Animated	Quiet
Intense	Relaxed
Realistic	Idealistic
Forceful	Gentle
Dramatic	Reserved
Direct	Subtle
Active	Passive
Analytical	Intuitive
Assertive	Submissive
Exuberant	Calm

The words listed above are divided into two columns because they are opposites. The words on the left describe "yang" traits; those on the right are "yin" traits. The yang is thought to be more forceful and active, the yin more gentle or passive.

The terms come from the ancient Chinese who believed that each person is a blend of two personalities, the yang and the yin. These opposite characteristics, when put together, make up the whole balanced person.

How much of your personality is yang and how much is yin? Look at the descriptive words you have circled in each category. Add up your yangs and your yins. Did you circle more traits in one column than in the other?

Nearly everyone is a composite of both, because within the framework of your "type," your moods may change. The tiger in the outside world may be a kitten at home (or vice-versa!). Colors have personalities, too. Every colortime has both yang and yin colors. You simply vary the shadings acording to the mood you want to convey.

If you want to express a yin mood, use the light to medium colors. If you want to express a yang mood, use the lighter or darker colors. Every hue ranges in mood from yin through yang. The lightest reds are pink. They are yin—soft, easy, non-threatening. The brighter reds are attention-getting yangs. The deeper wine-reds carry more authority and weight. They are also yang, but with added dignity.

You may not be aware that you are expressing a mood when you choose the colors of the clothing you are putting together, but you really are. Have you ever tried shopping on a day when you weren't feeling too good about yourself? Melancholy moods make it difficult to come home with anything in a color that you like. Try to do your shopping on a day when you are feeling "up," but if you can't always plan it that way, take your colortime swatches to at least help you avoid mistakes.

Wearing light colors—or deep or bright colors—all of the time can get monotonous. Just as you try to keep a balance in your personality, you should work toward balance in your clothing choices too. The words that you circle might change from month to month or even from day to day, depending on what's going on in your life.

Nothing can get a change of personality over faster to the rest of the world than a change of colors. **Bryan R.,** one of my clients, a bachelor in his mid-40's, had been dodging marriage to his ladyfriend, **Laura K.,** for about five years. She came to me to have her colors done and told me that she had had enough of this longstanding relationship with no engagement ring in sight. Laura was ready to make some changes in her life, but she needed a little encouragement.

She started by bringing some crossover true reds and orange blossoms into her sunlight palette to liven up the light greys and beiges she often wore. She had lovely hazel eyes with lots of blue-green in them. I suggested teal, a color she had never worn before, to enhance her eye color. She had always used pale aquas—pretty for lingerie and soft summer dresses—but she needed more pizazz for her new color personality.

I also suggested that she weave several blonde shades, ash and gold-beige, into her mousey-brown hair to get some color variation next to her skin.

I'm sure you've guessed the end of the story. They were married in a matter of months . . . Laura in a teal dress, Bryan in a light grey suit (with a teal tie). Bryan said he knew his days were numbered when she started to add more yang touches to her wardrobe!

At one time, yang traits were considered exclusively masculine, and yin characteristics were women's territory. Today we are less apt to classify color meanings by sex. Men are less reluctant to reveal their gentler side and women less afraid to exhibit assertiveness. Men wear pastel pink shirts and still come across as very masculine, and women can wear dark, tailored pants without losing their femininity.

Yang and yin colors can be combined. It is more difficult than staying with just one mood, but again, the secret is balance. An aubergine business suit in a very tailored mood can be softened by a mauve blouse with a ruffle at the neck. The suit is yang; the blouse is yin. It is true that most male styles are yang, but occasionally some yin breaks through. I have seen many macho types like **Burt Reynolds, Kenny Rogers,** and **Clint Eastwood** on formal evenings with ruffled yin pastel dress shirts under their yang black tuxedos. Can you imagine those he-man types ever wearing a ruffled shirt with a pair of jeans? Yet it's perfectly acceptable for formal wear. They're probably the last of the holdovers from the days of powdered wigs and satin waistcoats.

The yang navy blazer can be worn with a light blue shirt for a touch of yin contrast. When you change colors to suit changing moods, be sure your choice suits the occasion. A kelly green T-shirt may be great on a golf course, but all wrong in a dignified courtroom.

Most performers know how to use color to get their messages across. When **Olivia Newton-John** first performed on stage, she wore floaty, feminine fashions in the delicate shades of her Sunlight colortime. As her musical career was channeled into a more dynamic, assertive direction, she switched to brighter yang reds and blacks.

Sometimes one color says it all. **Johnny Cash** appears long-suffering and sober in yang black without a trace of color. **Carol Channing** sparkles in white gowns, and **Michael Jackson** often wears creamy white suits and shirts to set off his warm Sunset coloring. **Steve Martin** has used white suits as a trademark, and **John Travolta's** white suit created a worldwide fashion trend.

Flip Wilson told me that when he wears white he knows he's going to "knock the audience dead." White represents his highest level of energy and even when not performing, he always wears a touch of white for energy. Interviewing him was fantastic—he has a great sense of color.

He is a very definite Sunrise person with rose-brown skin and deeper hair and eyes. His living room is done in the vibrant Mediterranean blues and greens that he finds calming and soothing. He says about the only blues he doesn't like are the ones that people sing! He also likes rose-beiges and brown in his clothing, not only because they relate to his coloring but because he sees brown as the source of all things that grow and flourish.

As my interview drew to a close, I had to ask Flip one more question .... "What is Geraldine's favorite color?" Geraldine answered with, "Honey, Flip loves white and blue because he's cool, but Geraldine loves red and orange because she's hot!" Flip is Sunrise, but Geraldine is definitely Sunset.

Highly shiny metallics are very attention-getting yangs and are often used for theatrical effects. Broadway and Hollywood producer **Hillard Elkins** told me the story of how a chorus girl became a star by changing the color of her costume. During the production of "Golden Boy," starring **Sammy Davis, Jr.,** a scene that should have worked didn't.

Hilly asked the set designer to go for some brighter colors in the costuming—to "heat it up and add some gold for excitement." The designer did just that and put a very talented chorus girl in unforgetably slinky gold lamé pants. The scene magically came to life, and **Lola Falana** rose to stardom in the show.

You may feel that some physical liability limits the colors you can wear. Don't let the fact that you're heavier than you'd like to be commit you to a life of the "blahs." You don't have to wear dark yang colors all the time to reflect your yang moods—add a touch of brightness from your palette, preferably close to the face, to give you a spark.

If you have light coloring, especially in the Sunrise palette, you may feel overwhelmed by the brighter colors in your colortime. A touch of those colors in a tie, a scarf, or a piece of jewelry, or, for women, make-up shades can be a way to experience a wider range of your palette. The same is true for light skins in the Sunset colortime.

Shy or reserved people often have trouble handling the brighter yang shades for obvious reasons. But color can work to your advantage if you're shy—use a touch of a bright yang color and people will be drawn to you. At a party, you won't have to break the ice first—someone else will, because colors work like a magnet to draw others to you.

I had a student once say to me, "I'm a yang personality in a tiny yin body and my yang is dying to get out!" If you are a little person with a dynamic personality you can relate to that. A popular TV actress famed for her maternal role on a hit series has created a peachy yin ambiance in her home, except for her bathroom, which is done in gleaming yang black, has mirrors everywhere, and "disco" lights in the floor!

Interiors have personalities, too. A contemporary room done in a predominantly yang mood would be a room of strong contrasts, such as a charcoal grey flannel-covered sofa against pearl grey walls and carpeting, with strong accents of true red. Chrome, glass, and lacquered surfaces would be in sharp contrast to the matte grey flannel. Colorful abstract paintings, large paisleys, or bold prints are also yang—they make dramatic statements, as do high-tech designs and plastics.

A room done in a yin mood would be much less dramatic. Its colors would be quieter. Contrasts would be subtle. Smaller prints, lace curtains, and traditional decor and artwork are yin. A country kitchen with gingham curtains at the window is yin. A young girl's room done in soft, sunny yellows with a canopied bed and fluffy eyelet pillows is yin.

Yang and yin can be combined in a room. It is more difficult to combine them than to stay with just one mood, but again, the secret is balance. Just as with personality, one type will dominate. Never split a room down the middle or you will wind up with a room with a split personality. Dominance and subordination are the key—approximately 75 percent should be one type, and 25 percent the other. A mixture of moods and styles is called "eclectic" and may combine contemporary and antique pieces, but one mood should dominate.

Power Colors

A lot of attention has been given recently to color in clothing for business. I do agree with the "wardrobe engineers" who say that dark shades carry authority. The darker, basic yang colors carry more weight and convey an aura of power. The most powerful colors for men are navy, and dark or medium grey. Solid black for daytime is considered somber in men's suits and is associated with undertakers. A touch of black in slacks, sweaters, or ties works for daytime, but black suits are for more formal wear.

There is still a hint of country associated with brown. It is dark and dependable, and solid as the earth, but some men in large cosmopolitan areas stay away from it because they do not feel it is "citified" enough. They will go for it in leather or suede, but not in a suit or jacket.

Among the stars dressed for films by costume designer **Vicki Sanchez** are **Marsha Mason, Valerie Perrine, James Caan, Jack Nicholson, Jon Voight,** and **John Travolta.** She told me that in costuming for serious, powerful roles, she uses grey and navy.

But she says that brown could be used for power on the man who is trying to disarm everyone into thinking that he is just a "good ole boy" before he comes in for the kill (sounds like **J.R.** on "Dallas"!).

She uses nondescript washed-out tints on insipid, powerless characters.

Vicki works closely with the art directors and set designers on films and often uses chips of the wallpaper and paints to be sure that the clothes are compatible with the setting. She uses the colortime swatches as an aid in placing her clients in flattering, coordinated colors.

Women accept more color than men, but they also prefer browns in leather, suede, and furs. Because of this outdoorsy association of brown, you rarely see a formal dress in that shade and many women prefer brown for sportswear. Women have a greater color range to use in expressing power.

For women, the most powerful crossover basic shades, which work for every colortime palette, are:

Black—still considered   Navy
    the most sophisticated   Medium and dark grey
Medium and deep taupes   Wine, aubergine, raisin,
Deep evergreen   and brown (terre brun)

Power colors for PM palettes include paprika, bordeaux, terra cotta, deep tans, deep khaki, and avocado. Middays can use sages, bark, and chestnut, but the AM palette has to be careful of combining these earthy tones with AM colors. If you like those colors (and you usually don't), limit their use to touches. AM's may also use cocoa and bittersweet.

The lighter neutrals of sand, beige, light tans and greys, and light khakis and camels are not as powerful for either sex as the deeper values are, but they are appropriate substitutes in summer or in warm climates. Although in the most conservative areas, or in the south, a blue striped seersucker is acceptable for summer wear, I steer my clients to other summer-weight fabrics because I feel that it's difficult to look powerful in a suit that invariably looks like you slept in it!

I have done many corporate seminars on suitable clothing for business men and women. The president of a large company called me in to try to upgrade the image of his sales force. His particular problem was that most of his salespeople were accustomed to the casual Los Angeles lifestyle and their clothing colors were just not credible for selling a prestige service, especially in conservative northeastern states.

A few of the men were resistant to change (the women were not), but most of the men were receptive to changing their wardrobes to the more powerful, deeper tones. Their sales increased along with their credibility.

When I first moved to Los Angeles from the east coast, I was hired by a large Beverly Hills department store as a member of their executive staff with the title of Personnel and Floor Director. In addition to the hiring and firing (a terrible thing to have to do), I wore many other hats. Among my assignments were keeping the employees and the departments looking chic and up-to-date, and producing fashion shows.

Before I got the job, I had become so enamored of southern California's sunshine and lifestyle that I had bought lots of colorful new clothes to go along with my new life. I packed all of my dark basics—black, navy, browns, greys, etc.—off to a friend in New York.

When I was hired by the corporate personnel director, she told me that the required dress code consisted of the credible colors—you guessed it: black, navy, browns, and greys! Taupe and beige were acceptable in summer. Even in casual California, authority carries more weight in darker colors.

When clients come to me to have their colors done, I always explain that basic colors are the most practical. Some colors come and go, depending on fashion's whim, but basics are here forever. They are the dependable, serviceable standbys.

But basics can get boring, so for business wear I suggest a touch of pizazz near the face. For men, a touch of color in the tie, for women a blouse, jewelry, or scarf in a becoming color that radiates into the face can add just the right impact. Which colors are your impact colors? The ones in your colortime that are your true favorites—and the most becoming.

Try something different in combinations of power colors. Instead of the cliche-look of a brown suit with a beige blouse, try a brown suit with a rose blouse or navy with teal. The basic suit conveys the power and the impact color is used next to the face.

Altovese Davis (Mrs. Sammy Davis, Jr.) loves the warm earth-tones of her Sunset colortime—especially tomato reds used against creamy whites. She favors anything in warm pinks, and especially loves peach. When she adopts a conservative, businesslike look, she dips into the deeper shades of her palette.

Men, unfortunately, are much more limited than women in color choices, but there are general ways to break the sameness habit. Navy blazers are great basics, but why not try a pink oxford button-down (from your colortime) shirt, crossover grey slacks, and a tie that contains all three colors? The power of navy is predominant, but the pink adds a welcome creative touch.

Study the colors in your preferred colortime. Stretch your imagination and look for new combinations. The simplest method for finding interesting color combinations is to line all of your colors up and start playing with various possibilities. It will open you up to new and colorful ways of thinking, and it is really a very creative exercise. If you would like to keep the book intact and don't want to risk losing your cut-up colors, there is a form in the back of the book that you can use to send away for individual swatches in each colortime. There are swatches for each palette and they are divided into basic, neutral, and impact colors.

These are invaluable to have with you when shopping. You cannot remember a color exactly when you have walked even 36 inches away from it. You might get lucky and make the right choice, but then again, you might not. After it has been cut off the bolt or if it's on "final sale," right or wrong, it's yours forever!

Chapter 2 gave you the basics of color combinations and ideas on how to use colors together. If you need help in combining colors, refer to that list as a guide.

Power colors have been used effectively for many years in uniforms. Dark blue is the most universal of all uniform colors—it connotes all of the dependable messages of blue, but with the added strength and solemnity of black. In many areas, tans and khakis are issued in summer to replace the traditional dark blue policeman's uniforms. Although lighter in color, they still carry a military look and suggest aggressive action if necessary. Black shirts and uniforms are forbidding and scary. They remind us of SS men and Darth Vader and create fear rather than inspire confidence. Black is more acceptable as a uniform when trimmed with gold braid and worn with a white shirt.

As reported by **Garry Abrams** in the *Los Angeles Times*, "Colors and cravats have expanded the horizons of uniformity; with the bland no longer leading the bland, companies are being enticed into style variations and rainbow hues." He points out that approximately 10 million U.S. workers wear uniforms and that more service industries, such as real estate and banking firms, are getting into uniforms. One of the largest realtors in the nation is now putting red jackets on all salespeople, male and female. The jackets are a very yang red—definitely attention-getters, exciting and sales-stimulating.

The psychological message of a uniform seems to inspire consumer confidence. Airlines have long recognized the importance of inspiring the confidence of passengers by keeping flight crews in darker power colors. In recent years, some airlines deviated by dressing female flight attendants in cutesy miniskirts and garish color combinations, but that stopped when the women's movement started. How can a passenger have confidence in a Barbie doll? The pendulum has swung back to efficient-looking uniforms.

The nursing profession has veered away from sterile whites into pastels. However, at UCLA's Medical Center emergency room, the nurses decided to experiment in an effort to shed the "handmaiden" image and the subservient status that they feel is fostered by the medical profession's strict dress codes.

Instead of uniforms, they wear street clothes under white lab coats. Seventy percent of the patients polled felt that the nurses were warmer and more approachable, and that there was less of a barrier between them. It is interesting to note that they chose the white lab coat, which is still essentially a uniform, but one traditionally associated with doctors rather than nurses.

Surface Language Your First Impression

You never have another chance to make a first impression. Color can help you make that initial meeting something special. We often want to make a special first impression, especially on social occasions, but the most important occasion is likely to be a job interview.

Dr. Leonard Zunin, a psychiatrist, has written a book called, *"Contact: The First Four Minutes; An Intimate Guide to First Encounters."* In it, he talks about the four-minute time barrier, a time period in which initial human contact is established. If the initial reaction is negative, the eye and the mind start to wander to someone else.

When you are at a party and introduce yourself to a stranger, you begin a conversation. The first four minutes are spent in evaluating each other. We all do it, whether we admit it or not. TV commercials would have you believe that much of our negative reaction to others is based on the snowy dandruff on their shoulders, their yellow teeth, or the dark spots on their hands. As superficial as it seems, some of this is true. You do start to make judgments based on what you see—what Dr. Zunin calls your "surface language."

He states that "every color and mode of dress can influence the direction of contact regardless of whether or not the assumptions we make are correct." We dress not only to please our self-images, but to broadcast to others. Our tastes are vital clues to our personalities.

Job Interviews

Personnel interviewers judge you by your verbal, body, and surface language. To improve on that initial contact, I always make the following suggestions about color to anyone looking for a job.

1. Every business has a collective personality. Wear colors that are appropriate for that business. Obviously, a conservative power color like navy or grey will work best for an interview with a top level industry, attorney, or accounting office.

Alive With *Color*

Everything in nature works on a time clock—especially color. Writers, poets, painters and photographers often *describe* a particular time of day using the specific *shadings* we all associate with it.

Ask anyone, for instance, what colors they link with the word *sunset*. They will invariably say orange, gold, fiery reds, and (if they know the desert) hot purples. Think of *daybreak*, and your mind *sees* the cool grey light of dawn, clear blues and dewy greens. Think of *noon*, and you feel the full strength of the sun muting all colors to delicious pastels.

Sunrise (A.M.), Sunlight (Midday), and Sunset (P.M.)—these are color's *times*. Naturally enough, each of us is drawn to one of these groups of colors. We feel and look our best in them, because we each have a *colortime*, too.

Take the Colortime Quiz in the front of *Alive with Color* to discover your true colortime. You'll discover whether your natural affinity is to the colors of Sunrise, Sunlight or Sunset. Then learn how to use your colortime to dress your body and your surroundings, even please your psyche. Play with different palettes for different purposes, and really come alive...with color!

Leatrice Eiseman

Plate B

Photo: H. Armstrong Rob

Sunrise *(A.M.)*

The Sunrise (A.M.) colortime is the palette of a clear, dewy, fresh morning. This is the palette of the natural elements of air and water—transparent and frosty.

Ice Blue	Seafoam Green	Lavender Frost
Snow White	Mauve Morn	Celestial Blue
Aqua	Crystal Grey	Orchid Dawn

This colortime palette literally sparkles with royal and jeweled tones, like:

Amethyst	Aquamarine	Emerald Green
Opalescent Teal	Sapphire Blue	Windsor Blue
Regal Purple	Ruby Red	Fuchsia
Bright Turquoise		

The warm colors are pure and cooled-down:

Shell Pink	Cherry Red	Misted Rose
Rose-Pink Coral	Watermelon	Shocking Pink
Raspberry Glace	Sea Pink	

Your Kelly and Limeade greens are fresh, clean and bright, as are your Daffodil and Daybreak yellows.

Turn the page for all of the Sunrise colors.

The colors in this picture glisten with the serene, cool morning tones of Bright Turquoise, Celestial Blue, Snow White, plus the accents of Rose-Pink Coral and happy yellow flowers.

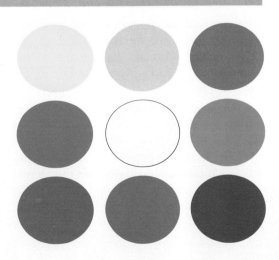

Plate C

Using Sunrise (A.M.) Colors

These fashion illustrations show you how the colors of the Sunrise palette can work to create a wonderful wardrobe with sparkling style. The combinations you seè are all drawn from the palette on the adjoining page. See Plates P and Q for more "Goof-Proof Combinations."

Some interior designers use renderings (a detailed sketch) to show a client how a projected color and design scheme will work. Stan Taylor, A.S.I.D., of Hollywood uses the Color Clock to help his clients feel comfortable and happy in their homes. At right Stan has used colors drawn from the Sunrise (A.M.) palette.

Fashion Illustration: Sharon Adams

Interior Illustration: Stan Taylor, A.S.I.D.

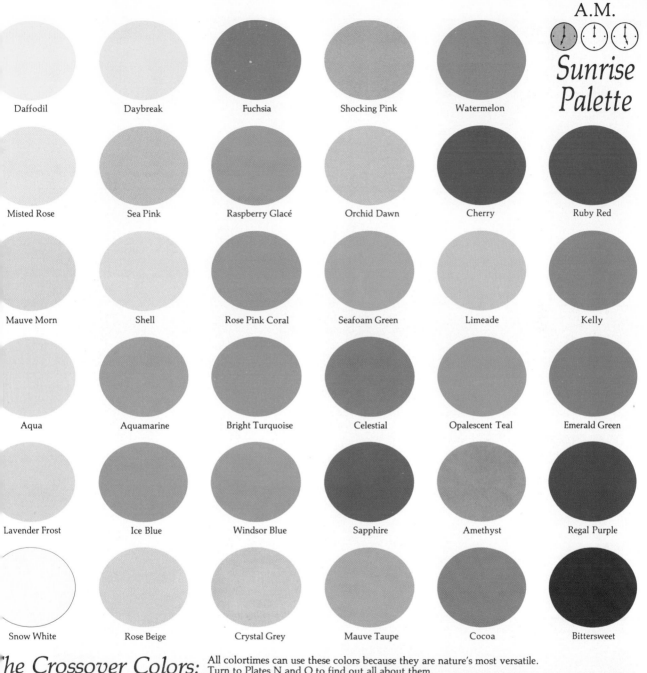

Daffodil	Daybreak	Fuchsia	Shocking Pink	Watermelon	
Misted Rose	Sea Pink	Raspberry Glacé	Orchid Dawn	Cherry	Ruby Red
Mauve Morn	Shell	Rose Pink Coral	Seafoam Green	Limeade	Kelly
Aqua	Aquamarine	Bright Turquoise	Celestial	Opalescent Teal	Emerald Green
Lavender Frost	Ice Blue	Windsor Blue	Sapphire	Amethyst	Regal Purple
Snow White	Rose Beige	Crystal Grey	Mauve Taupe	Cocoa	Bittersweet

The Crossover Colors:
All colortimes can use these colors because they are nature's most versatile.
Turn to Plates N and O to find out all about them.

Plate F

Sunset *(P.M.)*

The elements of fire and earth underscore the palette that speaks of a mellowed, golden evening. Warm tones are prevalent, from the spices of Cinnamon, Paprika, and Curry to the earth tones of:

Brick Red	Bordeaux
Bronze	Terra Cotta
Camel	Harvest Gold

Your greens are:

Bay Leaf	Hunter
Dill	Avocado
Khaki	

And, your blue-greens are cooled to deep twilight teals. More cool colors in your palette are:

Heathered Purple	Peacock
Lilac Dusk	Antique Turquoise
Cadet Blue	Dusk Blue
Smoke Grey	

Your pinks are dusted and warm, like Ash Rose and Coral Dust.
   Turn the page for all of the Sunset colors.

The fire colors of your palette are seen in this magnificent sunset of geranium and tomato reds, burnt orange, honeyed gold, and apricot against a periwinkle sky and purpled horizon.

Using Sunset (P.M.) Colors

These fashion illustrations show you how the colors of the Sunset palette can work to create a terrific wardrobe with excitement and flair. The combinations you see are drawn from the palette on the adjoining page. See Plates R and S for more "Goof-Proof Combinations."

This detailed sketch, or rendering, at right, was done by Hollywood interior designer, Stan Taylor. Stan frequently uses the same sketch in different colortimes to show clients the different moods color creates. Here he has used a combination of colors from the Sunset (P.M.) colortime palette.

Fashion Illustration: Sharon Adams   Interior Illustration: Stan Taylor, A.S.I.D.

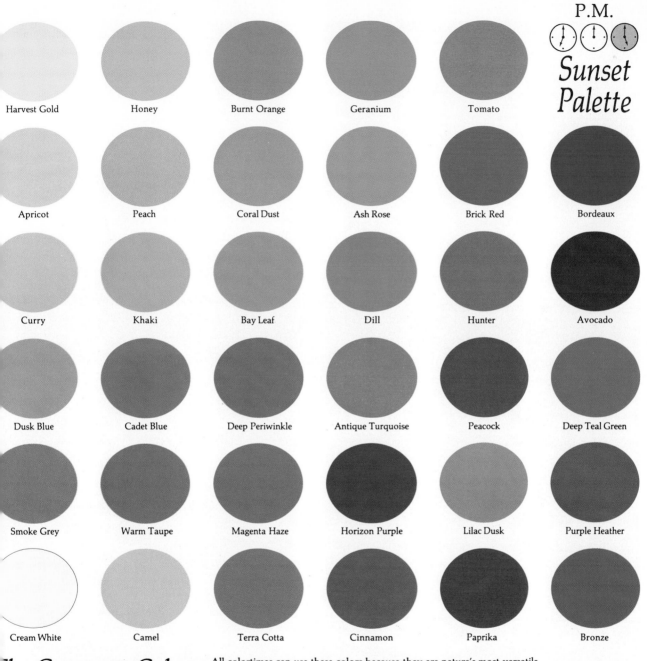

Harvest Gold	Honey	Burnt Orange	Geranium	Tomato	
Apricot	Peach	Coral Dust	Ash Rose	Brick Red	Bordeaux
Curry	Khaki	Bay Leaf	Dill	Hunter	Avocado
Dusk Blue	Cadet Blue	Deep Periwinkle	Antique Turquoise	Peacock	Deep Teal Green
Smoke Grey	Warm Taupe	Magenta Haze	Horizon Purple	Lilac Dusk	Purple Heather
Cream White	Camel	Terra Cotta	Cinnamon	Paprika	Bronze

The Crossover Colors:
All colortimes can use these colors because they are nature's most versatile.
Turn to Plates N and O to find out all about them.

Plate I

Plate J

Photo: Herb Eise

Sunlight *(Midday)*

The Sunlight (Midday) colortime is the palette of the sun-drenched noon hours. Colors are softened and slightly muted by the intensity of light everywhere. But they are filled with the sun's intensity, not paled. The warm shades are delectable:

Peach Melba	Mocha	Bisque
Buttercream	Lemonade	Creme Caramel
Melon	Strawberry Cream	Orange Blossom
Banana	Raspberry Sherbet	Vanilla

Your cool shades start with China Blue and include:

Delft	Mauve	Teal
Limoge	Jade	Wisteria
Wedgwood	Celadon	Lilac
Grape	Creme de Menthe	Mint
Plum Cordial	Soft Turquoise	Sage
Orchid		

Turn the page for all of the Sunlight colors.

The colors in this photograph of the Grand Canyon at Midday pulse with the subtle shadings of mauve, plum, chestnut, and grape combined with neutral grey, taupe and sage.

Using Sunlight (Midday) Colors

These fashion illustrations show you how the colors of the Sunlight palette can create a wardrobe with versatility and creative style. The combinations you see here are drawn from the palette on the adjoining page. For more "Goof-Proof Combinations," see Plates T and U.

Stan Taylor, A.S.I.D., rendered this color sketch, at right, of a room in the Sunlight palette. Midday colors are often the happy compromise for people with differing color tastes in the same household, since this palette uses subtle combinations gathered from both the A.M. and P.M. palettes.

Fashion Illustration: Sharon Adams   Interior Illustration: Stan Taylor, A.S.I.D.

Plate L

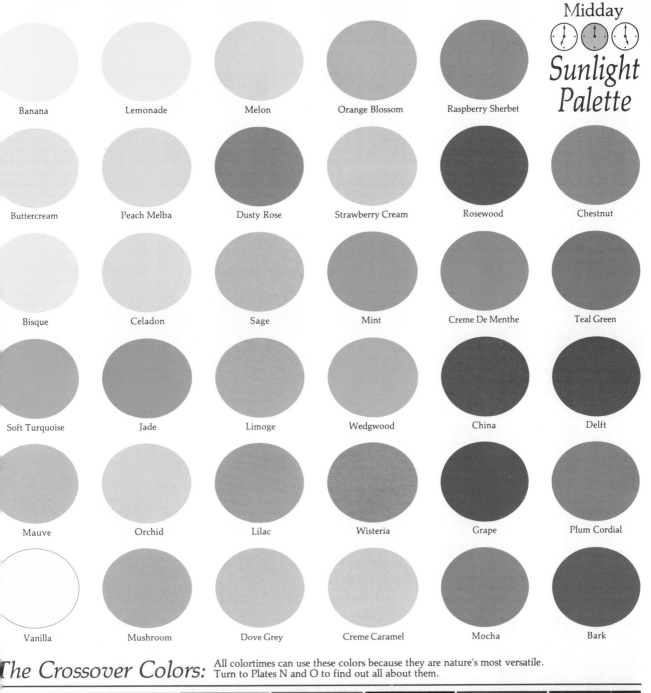

Midday Sunlight Palette

Banana	Lemonade	Melon	Orange Blossom	Raspberry Sherbet	
Buttercream	Peach Melba	Dusty Rose	Strawberry Cream	Rosewood	Chestnut
Bisque	Celadon	Sage	Mint	Creme De Menthe	Teal Green
Soft Turquoise	Jade	Limoge	Wedgwood	China	Delft
Mauve	Orchid	Lilac	Wisteria	Grape	Plum Cordial
Vanilla	Mushroom	Dove Grey	Creme Caramel	Mocha	Bark

The Crossover Colors:
All colortimes can use these colors because they are nature's most versatile.
Turn to Plates N and O to find out all about them.

Plate M

The Crossovers: *Nature's Most Versatile Colors*

In nature's "grand design" these colors appear everywhere. They go with all of the colortime palettes

Sunlight Yellow

Who doesn't love a bright, sunny day? This is the fun-loving tint that always adds a touch of warmth and cheer.

U.S. Department of Agriculture

Lori Eiseman

Taupe

(Greige) A combination of grey and beige, this is the perfect neutral. It's also known as mushroom, fawn, and otter because these shades blend so naturally into a wooded environment.

True Red

The balanced, bright floral color adds pizazz wherever it appears. Whether in a landscape, in a room, or on you, it's an energetic accent.

U.S. Department of Agriculture

Sky Blue

Against the beautiful back drop of blue sky, our eyes and minds are accustomed to seeing nature's myriad of colors—from red tulips and lavender hyacinths to yellow jonquils.

Nav

Dark navy blue is seen in depth of a deep body of wat Every sailor looks good in a na blue uniform and the wo knows that everything goes w the blue of blue jea

Terre Brun

This elegant French phrase means "dirt brown." But the tones of soil and wood make wonderful neutral and basic shades. Every shoot that emerges from the earth is poignant against brown.

U.S. Department of Agriculture

Plate N

Lori Eise

Evergreen

Stately evergreen is one of Mother Nature's most faithful shades. Wherever she arranges her flowers, she never forgets green. Have you ever denied a home to a lush plant because its green leaves didn't go with your color scheme? Of course not.

Robert Hickey

Sand

Look for the lightest beige-grey taupes in the sandstone of buildings, the wet sand and pebbles of beaches. Once you discover the terrific taupes, especially as an accessory color, you'll always want them in your closet.

Deep Wine

The deepest and most elegant of the reds, this color is as delicious as the vine-ripened fruit which inspired it. Every year is a good year for this timeless vintage shade.

Photo courtesy W. Atlee Burpee and Company

Pearl Grey

The lightest, most neutral grey of a snowy sky is also seen in the very first light of dawn. It's an undertone to the blue sky, and adds subtle depth to the blue-grey dusk.

Raisin

A brother to brown and a first cousin to wine and aubergine, raisin is the slightly purpled brown with an undertone that reminds us of the fruit from which it came.

Grey Flannel

The deeper, conservative classic is as solid as granite. Its understated elegance is an excellent foil for bright and light contrast.

Robert Hickey

Aubergine

In French it means eggplant, in clothing and interiors it means a classic deep purpled maroon. It blends tastefully into many color schemes.

Black

It's a perfect background for vivid contrast in clothing or interiors. Charcoal grey is so close to black, it can be used in the same dramatic or dignified ways.

Herb Eiseman

Photo courtesy W. Atlee Burpee and Company

Plate O

Sunrise (A.M.) *Goof-Proof Combinations*

The twenty-four combinations illustrated below are among the best "goof-proof" possibilities in the Sunrise palette. Some are classic and conservative, appropriate for a business suit, like monochromatic Grey Flannel and Crystal Grey. Others are more creative and fun, better for a bathing suit, like Sunlight Yellow and Limeade. Choose whatever combinations suit your needs, but use these suggestions to open yourself up to new possibilities. For example, one of the best ways to recycle a favorite navy jacket is to wear it with an emerald blouse or a touch of emerald in your tie. It will seem new again to you and everyone who sees it.

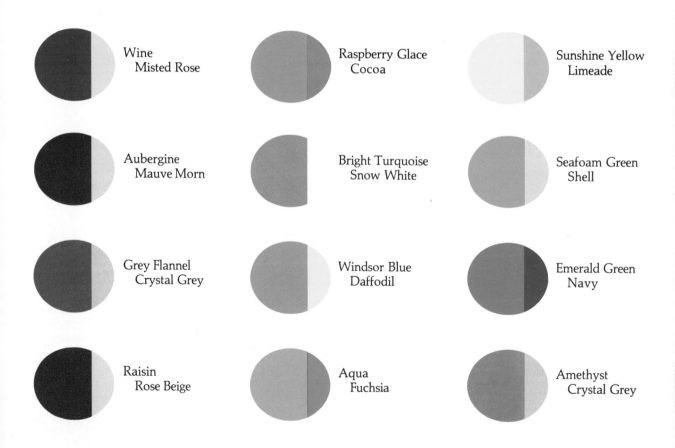

Wine
Misted Rose

Raspberry Glace
Cocoa

Sunshine Yellow
Limeade

Aubergine
Mauve Morn

Bright Turquoise
Snow White

Seafoam Green
Shell

Grey Flannel
Crystal Grey

Windsor Blue
Daffodil

Emerald Green
Navy

Raisin
Rose Beige

Aqua
Fuchsia

Amethyst
Crystal Grey

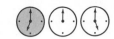

If you want to stretch your budget, use neutrals and basic colors. Make taupe, beige, grey, or deep basic shades like aubergine, raisin, wine, brown, navy, and charcoal part of your combinations. They are all classics that will work especially well as accessories for many colors.

For successful balance, one color is dominant, the second subordinate and the third an accent. Any color in your palette's combinations may be the dominant, subordinate or accent color. See Chapters 2, 3 and 4 for a complete discussion on using more than three colors together, plus additional "how-to's" for clothing and interiors.

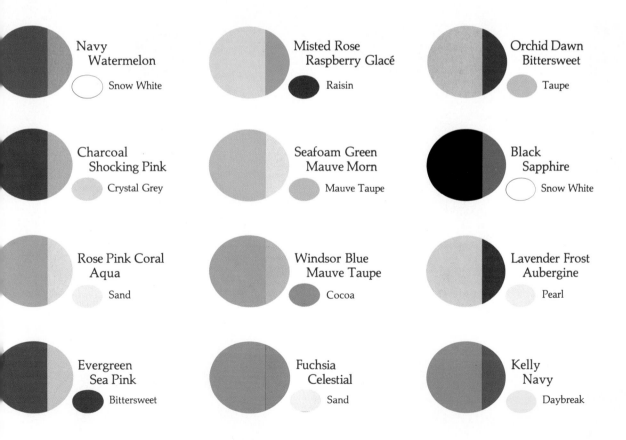

Navy
Watermelon
Snow White

Misted Rose
Raspberry Glacé
Raisin

Orchid Dawn
Bittersweet
Taupe

Charcoal
Shocking Pink
Crystal Grey

Seafoam Green
Mauve Morn
Mauve Taupe

Black
Sapphire
Snow White

Rose Pink Coral
Aqua
Sand

Windsor Blue
Mauve Taupe
Cocoa

Lavender Frost
Aubergine
Pearl

Evergreen
Sea Pink
Bittersweet

Fuchsia
Celestial
Sand

Kelly
Navy
Daybreak

Sunset *(P.M.) Goof-Proof Combinations*

The twenty-four combinations illustrated here are among the best "goof-proof" possibilities in the Sunset palette. Some are classic and conservative—best for a business suit—like monochromatic Terra Cotta and Camel. Others are more fun—great for a jogging suit—like Paprika and Peacock. Choose whatever combinations suit the occasion, but try to use these suggested combinations to open yourself up to all the possibilities of your palette. For example, the best way to update khaki pants is to wear them with a brick red shirt. You'll have instant pizazz!

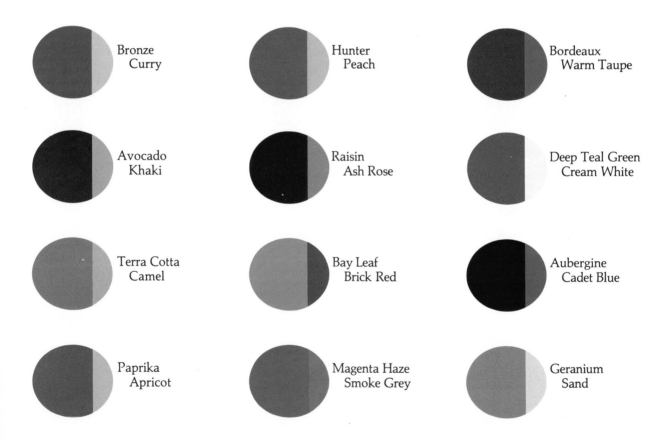

Bronze
Curry

Hunter
Peach

Bordeaux
Warm Taupe

Avocado
Khaki

Raisin
Ash Rose

Deep Teal Green
Cream White

Terra Cotta
Camel

Bay Leaf
Brick Red

Aubergine
Cadet Blue

Paprika
Apricot

Magenta Haze
Smoke Grey

Geranium
Sand

If you want to stretch your budget, use neutrals and basic colors. Make
~~taupes~~, tans, beiges, greys, or deep basic shades like aubergine, raisin, wine,
~~brown~~, navy, and charcoal part of your combinations. They are all classic colors
~~that~~ will work especially well as accessories.

For successful balance, one color should be dominant, the second subordinate
~~and~~ the third an accent. Any color in your palette's combinations may be the
~~dominant~~, subordinate or accent color. See Chapters 2, 3 and 4 for a complete
~~discussion~~ on combining more than three colors, plus additional "how-to's" for
~~your~~ clothing and interiors.

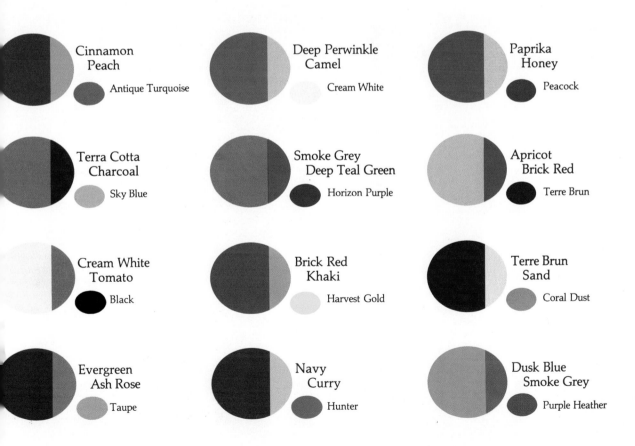

Cinnamon
Peach
  Antique Turquoise

Deep Periwinkle
Camel
  Cream White

Paprika
Honey
  Peacock

Terra Cotta
Charcoal
  Sky Blue

Smoke Grey
Deep Teal Green
  Horizon Purple

Apricot
Brick Red
  Terre Brun

Cream White
Tomato
  Black

Brick Red
Khaki
  Harvest Gold

Terre Brun
Sand
  Coral Dust

Evergreen
Ash Rose
  Taupe

Navy
Curry
  Hunter

Dusk Blue
Smoke Grey
  Purple Heather

Sunlight *(Midday) Goof-Proof Combinations*

The twenty-four combinations illustrated here are among the best "goof-proof" possibilities in the Sunlight palette. Some are classic and conservative—appropriate for a business suit—such as monochromatic Taupe and Tan or Mushroom and Bark. Others are more unusual and fun—great for a print—like Peach Melba and Mauve. Choose whatever combinations fit your mood or the occasion, but try to use these suggested combinations to open yourself up to all the possibilities of your palette. For example, the best way to perk up tired caramel "cords" (but still so comfortable) is to wear them with a Raspberry Sherbet sweater. That's a delicious combination!

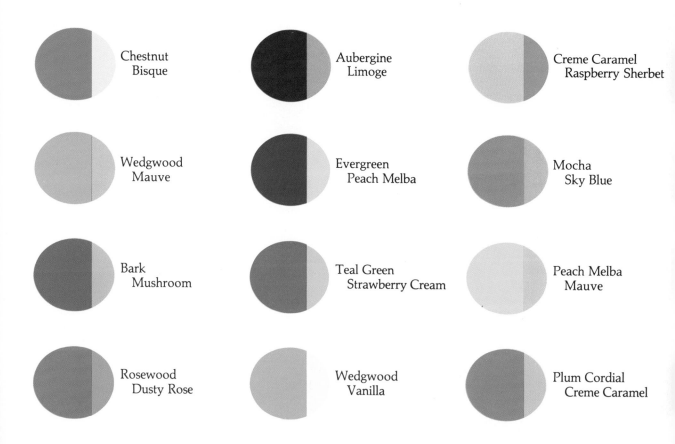

Chestnut
Bisque

Aubergine
Limoge

Creme Caramel
Raspberry Sherbet

Wedgwood
Mauve

Evergreen
Peach Melba

Mocha
Sky Blue

Bark
Mushroom

Teal Green
Strawberry Cream

Peach Melba
Mauve

Rosewood
Dusty Rose

Wedgwood
Vanilla

Plum Cordial
Creme Caramel

If you want to stretch your budget, use neutrals and basics. Make taupe, tan, ·ige, grey, or deep basic shades like aubergine, raisin, wine, brown, navy and ·arcoal part of your combinations. They are all classics that work especially well · accessories.

For successful balance, one color should be dominant, the second ·bordinate, and the third an accent. Any color in your palette's combinations ·ay be the dominant, subordinate or accent color. See Chapters 2, 3 and 4 for a ·mplete discussion on coordinating more than three colors, plus additional "how-·'s" on putting attractive combinations into your wardrobe and environment.

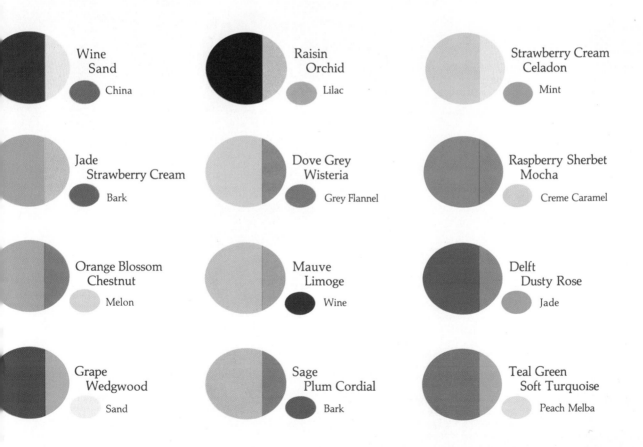

Color Wheel

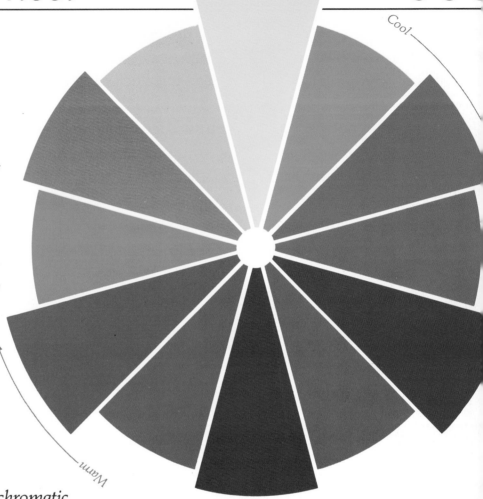

Warm and Cool Colors

Red, yellow, and orange, are associated with warmth. Blue, green, and purple (violet) are associated with coolness. But changing an undertone can change the temperature. Blue-reds are cooler than yellow-reds. The redder the purple, the hotter it gets. Blue-greens are cool, but the closer to yellow, the warmer green gets. Every colortime palette has both warm and cool tones, but Sunrise glistens primarily with the coolness of water and air; Sunset radiates mainly with the warmth of fire and earth. The Sunlight palette shares the subtle shadings of both. See the Colortime palettes to find your best warm and cool colors.

Monochromatic

This scheme *uses just one hue in varying shades* or tints—for example, a Sunrise bright turquoise, aquamarine, and aqua; or shocking and shell pinks from the same palette.

Analogous (Related)

These colors adjoin each other on the wheel. They are safe to use together because they are closely related, such as warm reds, oranges, and yellow. To expand your family, add a touch of the adjoining yellow-green. For example: the multi-colored Sunset combination of Geranium, Apricot, Terra Cotta, Gold and Honey, accented with a touch of Dill. Vary your shadings and allow one color to dominate.

Complementary (Contrastin

These are the colors which lie directly opposite to each other on the wheel. They intensify each other. A red rose seems eve redder against a green leaf. Strong contras scream for attention (such as the orange a bright blue detergent boxes in the market) Lightening or deepening one or both of th hues can be subtly pleasing, as in the Sun palette combination of Peach Melba and China Blue.

The colors on the wheel are gathered fr all three palettes. For the most harmoniou combinations in your colortime, see Chap 2 and the "Goof-Proof combinations" in Plates P, Q, R, S, T and U.

Plate V

Color in Interiors

Your home, no matter how large or small can be transformed into something wonderful and comfortable through the use of color. Turn to Chapter 3 and find out how you can decorate with color flair.

Celanese House

A youthful, fun approach that combines all palettes—dominant *A.M.* Sapphire and Pure White on floors, walls and table; fabric coverings in Midday Peach Melba with a dollop of P.M. Burnt Orange. Photo courtesy Celanese Corporation

Sears Poppy Festival

The clean impact of a bedroom done in analogous clear pinks, bittersweet, brown and white, particularly pleasing in the Sunrise *AM* palette.

Photo: Sears Roebuck and Company

Thomasville Chestnut Carpet, Mauvey Pillows

The Grand Canyon colors of the *Sunlight* (Midday) palette—chestnut, sand accented with an analogous mixture of pillows in mauves, grapes, and soft blue.

Photo: Thomasville Furniture Industries Inc.

Color in Interiors

People have always been fascinated with color and used it as a part of their surroundings. Skillful interior designers understand the enormous impact of color. Turn to Chapter 2 to discover dozens of *Goof-Proof Color Combinations* you can use in your own home.

Thomasville Pine and Bordeaux Dining Room Setting

The warmth of the carpet, golden pine furnishings, Bordeaux sofas and walls, with a touch of Magenta Haze on the table shows a unique use of the Sunset (*P.M.*) palette.
Photo: Thomasville Furniture Industries Inc.

Sears Brick and Blue Den

The opposite complementary shadings of Brick Reds, Browns and Peacock Blue set the cozy mood of this Sunset (*P.M.*) den.
Photo: Sears Roebuck and Company

Thomasville Evergreen and Sand Bedroom

A sophisticated bedroom of crossover Evergreen and Sand that works for *all* palettes. The pillow colors can be varied according to your tastes.
Photo: Thomasville Furniture Industries

Plate X

2. If you're going for a job with a glamour industry, women can (and should) wear trendy shades to accent power colors. You will let them know that you know what is happening in the fashion field. Men can bring interesting colors into shirts and ties. Don't wear something unimaginative like a white shirt and a solid tie.

3. Men should avoid dark shirts and light ties with light suits for conservative companies. You'll look like something out of an old **Edward G. Robinson** or **George Raft** movie—too gangsterish and slick, especially for banking, insurance, and accounting firms.

4. Chances are you'll be one of many applicants. Try to make yourself a little more "memorable" by using some interesting conversation piece of color. For women, this is easy—a piece of jewelry, a smart scarf at the neck, or an impact color in the blouse can help make you stand out from all the other applicants. For men, an interesting tie with a touch of color and a pastel shirt will have to suffice, preferably in your signature colors, as described below.

5. Avoid colors that are generally turn-offs or "tacky" brilliant. Overly vivid purples, brilliant oranges, garish yellow-greens, for example. You'll be memorable, but for the wrong reasons.

6. Wear colors that repeat or enhance your hair, skin, and eye color. For example, if you have Midday streaked blonde-brown hair, hazel eyes that combine blue, green, and brown, and variegated rose and beige skin, wear a beige suit for your hair color, a blue-green shirt for your eyes, and a tie or scarf of beige and blue-green with a touch of dusty rose. These are your "signature" colors—a wonderful way to capitalize on your own coloring and make you stand out from the crowd. Everyone has a personal color signature. If you have AM black hair, black skin, and very dark eyes, there are always other undertones present.

Alive
With Color

For your coloring I would suggest black for hair and eyes, and since dark black skin often has an undertone of blue in it, a bright, clear blue for contrast. A touch of white could enhance the white of the eye.

If you have trouble coming up with color combinations, Goof-Proof combinations in Chapter 2 can help you expand your imagination.

One of the best-dressed men in Hollywood often utilizes his signature colors. When I talked to **Robert Wagner** on the set of "Hart To Hart," I couldn't help but notice that his shirt matched his deep blue-grey eyes perfectly (his favorite color is blue) and that his tan suit complemented his handsomely tanned skin. His tie combined both shades with a touch of off-white for contrast. His colortime is Sunset.

What Your Place Says About You

Your home is an extension of you. It is your territory and reflects part of your personality. When I visit a client's home, I always look for clues that might help me to guide their color choices. When people come to your home, they get a sense of you from the moment they walk through the door.

A colorless house has an austere, uninviting impact. Too many colors give a disorganized, jumbled impression. Too many cool colors with no warmth make a house unfriendly and aloof. Warm colors are instantly hospitable. If the colors get too warm or hot, however, the atmosphere can be overpoweringly friendly.

Try to look at your setting with an objective eye. Do your colors really reflect you? Are you content and comfortable with your choices? Environmental psychologists tell us that people should live in environments designed to avoid anxiety-provoking colors. If you always feel slightly uneasy or uncomfortable in a particular room, the colors may be disturbing you.

Environments should enhance your psychological well-being. Expressing yourself in your surroundings is basic to your feeling of security—you feel "rooted." Self-expression through decorating a home is a form of therapy.

Working in an emotionally cold office can make you feel alienated, bored, and anxious. It's important to bring some personal belongings to work in order to feel comforted. Put a colorful photograph on your desk, or take a pet plant to work; anything to add a dash of color and help you feel less depersonalized in sterile surroundings.

I have a friend with a prolific green thumb. She has loaded her office with so many plants that you practically have to hack your way through with a machete. But it does create a delightful atmosphere of greenery and makes her feel more at home. She really relates to people who say, "It's a jungle out there!"

Communicating With Color

The Colors you choose for your personal and business stationery, business cards, flyers, and announcements all create an instant impression. They tell a story about you even though you are not actually present.

Most people will choose personal stationery in colors that blend with their favorite colortime. You can make your stationery part of your personal signature—a projection of your personal coloring.

Lynn Redgrave uses a creamy stationery embossed with a monogram several shades deeper than her beautiful burnished red hair. Lynn has that wonderfully unusual Sunset coloring of coppery hair, light cream skin with a peachy undertone, and peacock blue eyes. She tells me that she likes the earth tones and her favorite colors are autumn golds, dusky blues, and peaches, which are the undertones of her own personal coloring. She also favors dusky lilacs and creams, golden brown dogs, and honey-colored kittens!

Joan Collins favors peach-colored stationery. Peach invariably gives a message of instant warmth. Her stationery is a warm yin, but the characters she often plays are fiery yangs! At a fashion show she emceed recently, she wore a bright crossover true red suit with matching hat and I couldn't help but notice that her green eyes looked greener than ever against the complementary red.

For business stationery and cards, I suggest using the colors that best express the kind of business you're involved in. White is classic, of course, with black print for the letterhead. But it is rather ordinary, and certainly not as arresting as colors are. The tints used do not have to be blatant to be interesting.

If you want to convey the message that you are:

Cool, conservative, efficient	Light crossover neutral greys with contrasting darker grey, black, or deep wine print
Understated and cool, but more interesting	Light blue with navy print Light green with dark green print
Warmer, yet still understated	Creams and beiges with brown print Soft yellow with brown print
Fashion-oriented, but subtle	Interesting Midday combinations, such as lilac and mauve
Cosmetics-oriented	Flattering skin tones in all colortimes, such as roses, pinks, peaches, and mochas with appropriate print
Stimulating and attention-getting (for flyers and special mailing pieces)	Bright colors of both Sunrise and Sunset palettes are especially good for announcements of sports activities such as exercise and dance classes.

Bold, daring, and eyecatching	Combine the opposite palettes of Sunrise and Sunset for deliberate discord. Use complementary combinations like hot purple against yellow and no one will be able to ignore you!
Artistic and creative (florists, gift shops, designers, etc.)	Unusual color combinations always reflect a flair. Discord is less desirable here, because to a prospective client, this is a preview of your work. Use pleasing but colorful combinations from all palettes; Midday is the best choice.

I recently spoke at a Direct Mail/Marketing Association convention, where I was shown some fascinating material on the benefits of using colored and/or textured paper rather than pure white.

Test mailings included questionnaires, descriptive brochures, business reply cards and envelopes, order forms, and requests for contributions. Response rates for the colored/textured paper showed dramatic increases of from 7½ percent to 142 percent, underscoring the powerful force of color in the marketplace.

Marketing Messages

Market testing indicates that your eye rests on a product for approximately .03 seconds as you speed along the supermarket aisle. So the message that you get and the association that you make with the product must be instantaneous.

Low-cal sweeteners are in a pink pack to make them even sweeter. Fabric softeners are pastel to make them even softer. Bottled bleaches for even whiter whites are packaged in pure white plastic. In a recent television commercial for chlorine bleach, the kindly pure white-haired supermarket clerk wears a spanking white shirt made even whiter by the reflection of his sapphire-blue apron. The woman he is selling the bleach to is wearing a tattle-tale grey shirt and has dishwater blonde hair!

You learn to expect that an aerosol in a green can will freshen the air better than an aerosol in a black can, and you are less apt to buy furniture polish in a purple can than in a brown one that suggests the richness of the wood.

Companies like the **Corning Glass Works** in Corning, New York, do extensive testing to find out what your consumer preferences are and to provide you with them. **Estelle Rothstein,** Project Designer for Corning, says, "Style is important, but color is critical." She finds that the current trend is for the customer to choose groups of colors, rather than one specific color.

Interestingly, Corning has three classifications of color, which fit right into the three colortime palettes. The first features the PM earth tones of browns, rust, orange, and gold. The second includes the AM group of blues, lavenders, greens, aquas, pinks, and yellows, and the third has a country look that uses colors from each of the other two in variations of bands, plaids, and stripes of the Midday palette.

Estelle reports that color trends do change, but one has stayed constant over the years: the popular, identifiable Corning blue. About 10 to 15 percent of the population likes blue and are not swayed by what is popular; the preference is especially strong in New England. Among the majority of buyers, color trends have historically shifted approximately every six to eight years.

The fashion industry often separates color into groupings. In a recent showing of a knit collection by **Missoni,** the master colorist from Italy, the colors were divided into the three colortime palettes. The Sunset grouping was translated as: painted desert shades of earthy reds, warm greys, burnt coppers, pewter, and sandstone. The Sunrise colors were ocean greens and blues, ultramarines, and pink corals. The Sunlight palette contained various deliciously edible shades of mango, grape, passion fruit, and almond green.

Gold and silver in packaging give an aura of luxury and suggest quality. Wines, champagnes, and expensive chocolates are often foil wrapped. Yang black and gold used together are considered the ultimate in quality and sophistication.

Even simple little jelly beans are subject to market testing. Red and black have been found to be the most preferred, white and purple the least. Candy makers are advised not to include more than 4 percent of these colors in their packages.

Color has been known to increase productivity in industry. In a major manufacturing plant a colorful supergraphic was painted on a huge, formerly dull wall. Production increased by 8 percent. In addition, the restroom walls were painted a bilious green. That really got people back to their machines in a hurry!

At **20th Century-Fox Studios,** a large building housing many employees was subdivided into smaller, more congenial areas where several people work at desks in groupings. Each area in this vast space is separated by room divider panels in various bright colors for easy identification. One of the employees I questioned commented that the color is lively and helps to keep her "up." Vivid colors do stimulate people to activity. She also said that when she first went to work there she felt like a mouse in a maze and that the colors were the only way she could find her way back to her desk!

Color coding is a very effective way to keep office or home files organized for quick and easy recognition—especially at a distance. Stationery stores are full of colorful rainbows of red, green, blue, and yellow gummed dots and squares that can help you organize your life.

Offices and Waiting Areas

Prospective clients and customers start to make a judgment about what you have to offer them the moment they cross your threshold. The moment the door is opened your image is projected. You have to work even harder to overcome poor impressions if those first few moments of contact are not favorable (including the receptionist's welcoming smile and appropriate clothing!).

I often suggest to doctors, dentists, and therapists that their waiting rooms be done in calming colors. This is an ideal setting for the gentler Sunlight colortime and provides a good balance of warmth and coolness. The extremes of the brilliant Sunrise blues or greens or the fiery Sunset reds and oranges would not be a good choice because they may stimulate rather than subdue a nervous patient.

Attorneys, accountants, bankers, and business managers can use monochromatic neutral beiges, taupes, and wood finishes and feel confident that they are always in good taste. The message is understated, careful, safe. Too much blue or green in this type of setting without some touch of warmth could come across as too cold and impersonal. As the song goes, "You Gotta Have Heart," and that is what warm colors say to you.

Power colors are excellent for serious business. The business management offices of **Traubner, Flynn, Philpott, Murphy, and Kress,** in Century City, California, are done in deep crossover evergreen (a good color to associate with money), warm taupes, and a bit of navy, with touches of terra cotta and peach for needed warmth in a subtle print. This is a good, reassuring background message of responsibility and caring for their many top show business clients like **Warren Beatty, Goldie Hawn,** and **Paul Newman.**

We identify particular colors with certain names and products. Even if we cannot see the name on the package, we know that the neon yellow and red package contains **Kodak** film. We can spot a bright red and white striped box of chicken from the late colonel a half a block away, and that **Baskins-Robbins** ice cream store is always resplendent with dollops of ice-creamy colors.

You don't have to be part of a huge conglomerate to establish company colors. Just like school colors, for easy and interesting identification purposes, they're part of a company image. **St. Clair Pakwell,** of Wilsonville, Oregon, makes custom retail packaging and gift wrap.

They have established a PM logo of orangey-rusts, terra cotta, and "breen" (a warm green-brown) against off-white for company stationery and business cards, and have carried these colors into the home office. The business cards are put into tiny paper bags with the same colors—a really memorable touch.

Anna Mack, the art director, told me that they had a little trouble adjusting to the orangey tones, but after six years, it has proven "uplifting" during the winter months. She says that "Days and weeks of grey, dark exteriors make the orange tones a pleasant and cheery area in which to work."

If you need to make a choice about a business or personal color signature, choose the palette first and then use the combinations in the color section to help you make the decision.

Confessions of a Closet Organizer

I have spent years in clients' closets. Now that it's out in the open, I can tell you that once I get started on someone's closet, there is no stopping me. I'm like a scene out of one of those old Keystone Kop movies or a **Benny Hill** TV show where all of the characters flail their arms and run around nonstop.

There is nothing I like to do more for a client than to rearrange, weed out, sort out, and recycle. It's instant gratification for me and my client. I can also get some instant insight into a client's personality and lifestyle through the colors he or she wears. If you're like most people, opening your closet door and finding it neat, efficient, and attractive makes you feel so "together." Somehow, when your closet is organized, you feel as though your whole life is organized. (If only that were true!)

I could do a whole book on closets, but let's stick with the important points. The very best time to get your closet together is when you are redecorating or repainting. Everything is a mess anyhow, so a little more mess can't possibly hurt. You have to have everything out of the closet anyway, unless you're one of those sneaky people who repaints a whole house but never touches the 50-year-old wallpaper in the closet. I view my closets in much the same way my mother viewed clean underwear. You never know when you might be involved in an accident and get carted off to a hospital—and you just never know when someone is going to open the door to your closet!

The key to a wonderfully arranged closet is color. When you are really ready to get into it, the following guidelines can give you a plan of action:

1. Pull out anything you haven't worn in a year and put it on the bed.

2. Separate day clothes from evening clothes. Put them in different sections of the closet.

3. Keep all of the same kinds of clothing together. Blouses and/or shirts together, pants together, skirts together, suits, etc.

4. Arrange them all by color.

5. Throw away all your shoeboxes (unless you have x-ray vision) and put your shoes in see-through plastic containers. Writing on the outside of cardboard boxes doesn't work—you usually can't remember what the "black loafers" look like! Keep your shoes at eye level or above if possible, so that you don't have to crawl around on all fours groping for them.

6. Organize your handbags, sweaters, socks, and/or stockings, and underwear, and put them in see-through plastic containers. Especially stockings and socks—it really takes the frustration out of fishing through the black, browns, and navies when you keep them separated by color.

7. Try to get as much as possible out of bureau drawers and onto shelves so that you can see exactly what you have. I've discovered things in bureau drawers that my clients hadn't seen in years. If you don't see it, you don't use it. Haven't you ever brought something home from the store only to discover eventually that you had something just like it—that you had simply forgotten about it?

8. Get a piece of peg-board and assorted metal hanging hooks from your local hardware or building supply store. If your closet is big enough, put it up on a wall or on the back of a door. If you don't have the space, use a bedroom, bathroom, or dressing room wall. This is where you're going to hang your costume jewelry and belts—all by color on the metal hooks placed in the peg-board. This is also a good place to hang odd things that don't seem to go anyplace else.

9. Put a piece of thin foam rubber over some wire hangers and hang your scarves or ties from them. Arrange them by color. They won't slide off and you won't have to press the wrinkles out of your scarves every time you wear them.

The ideal closet has double-hung rods so that you can keep your blouses or shirts hanging above your pants and/or skirts. Since everything should be arranged by color, you can readily see what you have in each family of color. It is so much easier to see what goes with what.

To get back to that pile of clothes on the bed that you never wear, check them out to see why you aren't wearing them. Chances are that you have nothing to wear them with—they're usually the "bargains" that are not in your colortime.

If you're not wearing them because they are just a little out of date, (wide lapels, narrow lapels) but they're classic, decide if alterations are really worth it, or move them to another closet, or retire them permanently. I've caught some of my closaholic clients sneaking things back into the closet from that pile. When I confront them with the crime, they will often wail, "but I wore that to my high school prom!" (20 years before).

You don't have to be brutal about it. You can keep anything that has real sentimental value. But the whole point is to get organized and to give yourself more space.

As you continue to buy clothing in your preferred colortime palette, you will see how much easier and more practical it is to combine, mix and match, and enjoy your clothes as well as your colors.

Themes and Schemes—Weddings and Parties

Color is the most important part of what makes a party special. Using your colortime combinations can make a table setting, a floral display, or a wedding party memorable and harmonious. The colors create the ambiance (and the beautiful photographs) that everyone remembers.

Just as in decorating interiors, the Color Clock and the color wheel are the two circles that get your creative wheels turning. The first choice is always made by deciding on a colortime palette that will evoke the mood that you want to achieve.

Some of the most creative schemes I have ever seen have been at the parties that celebrate the premiere or "wrap-up" of a film. It is a real challenge to take a cavernous building like a sound stage and turn it into something magical. Movies have always been magical to me, and I am always impressed with the amount of creative ability that goes into making them.

Of course, it does help to have rooms full of props and professional set decorators available, but some of the simplest settings turn out to be the best. One of my favorites was the table setting for an informal "wrap-up" party after the completion of a western film. The tables were covered in gingham bed sheets used as tablecloths. Masses of orange-red geraniums in ordinary clay pots were used as centerpieces. The napkins were tomato-red bandanas. It was a warm and homey PM touch and it was wonderful in its simplicity.

You don't have to have a super-large budget if you use potted plants. You can go to your local nursery, choose whatever is in season and build your colortime scheme around it. A pot of chrysanthemums in the fall can be surrounded by autumn leaves and sunset colors.

Favorite objects, such as a collection of old bottles made blue with water and a drop of food coloring, each with one flower or a bit of baby's breath, can inspire an AM setting. A plain philodendron can be given some unexpected glamour with three or four delicate real or silk flowers tucked randomly into the plant for a soft Sunlight look. A glass bowl full of colorful marbles makes an ideal base to push stems down into to keep them secure. It also gives you a colorful kaleidoscope of whatever colortime pleases your fancy.

Weddings can be made even more beautiful by the use of the right color combinations. Since the wedding party needs to be dressed harmoniously, this is not the time for individual color choices, but the most important decision is: what colortime is going to be the dominant theme?

The bride, traditionally, gets to choose the colors. Ideally, she will confer with everyone involved, but in the final analysis, she gets to choose. Somebody has to have the last word. Invariably, the bride chooses her own favorite colortime. I've rarely seen it work any other way, unless there is a very domineering Mama or Mama-in-law involved.

Many grooms are now demanding equal say and playing a part in the whole process. Eventually (usually) everybody agrees and they all live happily ever after. However, it doesn't always happen that way. One couple asked me to arbitrate because they couldn't decide on wedding colors, furniture for the apartment, or the color of the car they were going to share.

He was a Sunset and she was a Sunrise and both were very definite about their likes and dislikes. They compromised on the Sunlight palette, which seemed to satisfy them both. They invited me to the wedding. A few weeks later, I was un-invited. It seems that colors were not the only thing they couldn't agree on.

Most everyone in the wedding party can find a color in the Sunlight palette that pleases them and its subtlety suits the occasion. Crossover colors are also a good compromise. Bridesmaids in wine or evergreen velvets and ushers in grey have become traditional in winter weddings.

Coordinate your flowers and table linens to go with the wedding party colors and everything will be beautiful. When you look back at the wedding pictures in years to come, it will be worth all of the effort.

I am reminded of one Hollywood wedding—the bride and the groom shall remain nameless—where the bride wore a lace dress that must have been worn in "Gone With The Wind." It was miles of blush-colored lace over an enormous hoop skirt. She also wore a huge picture hat.

There was barely enough room for her father to walk down the aisle with her, so he sort of trailed behind. It took the groom what seemed like a full five minutes to maneuver around the skirt with the big hoop, so that he barely reached her lips for the final kiss, and almost knocked her hat off.

Her attendants all wore whatever colors they chose—a variety of vivid colors. It was definitely not what you would call subtle.

Other Occasions

For confirmation parties, Sweet-16's, bar and bat mitzvahs, and other special events, the colortime used should be the one favored by the honoree. The colortime theme can start with the invitations and carry through the flowers and the rest of the decor.

If you are planning the party and the colortime used is not your favorite, keep an open mind. Fashion coordinators and interior designers learn how to please their clients and often use colors they don't find personally pleasing.

After the colortime is chosen, you decide on the dominant and subordinate colors within that colortime. Then you refer to the color wheel to decide on how you want to combine your colors. The procedure is much the same as it is in decorating a home. You must decide whether you are going to use:

> One dominant color *(monochromatic)*
> Two colors *(one dominant and the other subordinate)*
> Three colors *(one dominant, the second subordinate, the third, a touch)*
> Multicolors *(polychromatic)*

Remember that the analagous colors are easy to combine. The complementaries will be the most attention getting when used in the brightest intensities (good for the bubble gum set).

Don't let the terminology scare you. Go back to page **97** and look at the Goof-Proof combinations. I suggest to clients that they use a color board, much the same as the one described earlier. It really does help to use color swatches to represent linens, flowers, candles, etc.

You can use paint chips that approximate your choices, if you don't want to cut the book up, just to see how the combination will look. It really is a fun, creative, exercise. It's just like being back in kindergarten with your paste and baby scissors (the kind you could never cut with). It's also marvelous therapy after a long, harrowing day. You may like it so much that you continue to do paste-ups after your party is over and you're left with wonderful memories, a photo album, and, of course, the bills.

Cars and Colors

Your automobile is an extension of your personality—an unspoken, but clear message to the rest of the world. The passenger in the sleek black limousine conveys a powerful and important "yang" image. The macho driver aggressively darting in and out of traffic in a red Porsche probably fancies himself on the race course in LeMans.

Distinctive car styles and colors provide wonderful opportunities for living out fantasies. The husband of one of my clients, a retired 65-year-old, drives a vintage Mustang painted a bold tomato red. He had always driven cars of nondescript grey or tan to his job with an insurance company. These sedate, low-key vehicles were part of his very conservative image.

He told me that when he retired, he realized that it was "now or never." The "yang" in him could finally have its day. He chose tomato, the vivid red-orange in his Sunset colortime, because it makes him really come alive when he gets behind the wheel.

Another client enjoys spotting unusual personalized license plate messages. On a recent cross-country trip he noticed one that he especially liked (the driver as well as the message). As he drove along-side a cute little AM blue Volkswagen Rabbit, he saw that the driver was a cute little AM blue-eyed blonde. As she drove ahead, he noticed that her license plate read "Bunny." Was that her name, he wondered, or did it simply go with the "Rabbit"? Whatever the reason, her car was a strong reflection of her self-image.

If you're like most people, you choose your car color with great care and deliberation and, if you have a good range of choices, will choose it in your favorite colortime. We've come a long way from the days of Henry Ford who handled the question of car color for his original Model T's by telling his customers that they could have any color they wanted as long as it was black!

If you're the practical, thoughtful type who researches very carefully before buying, you might select your car's color on the basis of its safety factor. The most visible color is schoolbus-yellow. Orange shades also stand out, but at twilight or under foggy conditions, yellow, light beiges, cream, and white are more visible than orange. Yellow is strongly recommended for small compact cars because it visually increases their size. If you do drive a car in these highly visible colors, however, you'd better drive with care—you'll also be highly visible to the sharp-eyed highway patrol!

Some of the most popular shades of blue and brown are, unfortunately, among the least visible colors, and record high accident rates. Red cars would logically seem fairly safe because of the conspicuousness of the color, but they too rate high in accident statistics. Red appears darker at twilight, and under most street lighting, seems almost dark brown.

White and off-white are suggested for warm climates because their reflective qualities keep interiors cooler; dark colors absorb heat. If you have your car repainted, it's wise to choose a color that was standard for its make, model, and year. Choosing an off-color could lower its trade-in or resale value.

What color is *your* car? Your association with certain colors and the psychology of those colors—information in Part Two of this book—will help you understand your color choices of the past, and how they are likely to change in the future.

Part II

What Color Says About You

Chapter 5

Your "Shady" Past & "Brilliant" Future

Your Color Profile Quiz

The first part of this quiz deals with word association. Simply write the word or words that come immediately to mind. Do not change your original answer and do not linger over it. In the columns labeled "Pleasant," "Unpleasant," or "Indifferent," check your reaction to the colors listed. The words that you have chosen to describe the colors will help you to decide which column to check.

Colors	Word Association	Pleasant	Unpleasant	Indifferent
Royal Blue				
Navy				
Sky Blue				
Lavender				
Purple				

Colors	Word Association	Pleasant	Unpleasant	Indifferent
Yellow				
Orange				
Peach				
True Red				
Soft Pink				
Vivid Pink				
Wine				
Brown				
Rust				
Bright Green				
Forest Green				
Olive				
Blue-Green				
Aqua				
White				
Black				
Grey				
Beige				
Taupe				

Now answer these questions:

Are your choices influenced by whether the colors are currently fashionable?

_____

_____

_____

Do other people influence your choice of colors?

_____

_____

_____

In what cities and/or countries did you spend your childhood?

_____

_____

_____

What area of the world did your parents come from?

_____

_____

_____

Color Psychology Quiz

List your favorite colors:

_____

_____

_____

_____

List your least favorite colors:

_____

_____

_____

_____

Let's find out about your associations with color. Taking a quiz off the "top of your head" can tell you a lot about yourself.

Add up the checks under the "Pleasant," Unpleasant," and "Indifferent" categories on pages 160 and 161.

Analyzing Your Answers

Were most of your checks in the "pleasant" column? If so, you have a generally positive attitude toward color. You are probably enthusiastic, well-adjusted, and enjoy many different colors. You are flexible and open to new experiences. You are likely to have been encouraged to play with crayons and paints as a child and loved it.

If more of your answers were in the "unpleasant" category, you are somewhat closed to trying new colors and color combinations. You are likely to be conservative, a bit opinionated, and have a difficult time expressing yourself with color. Someone may have criticized you when your colors ran over the outlines of the drawings in your coloring book, and that same someone may have told you which colors to use where. But where there's life, there's hope. As you begin to understand why you have so many unpleasant associations, you will open up to the magical world of color.

If most of your answers were in the "indifferent" category, you've probably not had the opportunity to experience the creative use of color. Perhaps you attended schools that emphasized the basics— where art was given low priority and most of your time was spent on the three "R's." You may be indecisive about choosing colors simply from lack of experience. You definitely need some pizazz in your life!

If your answers were equally divided between "pleasant" and "unpleasant," with few or no "indifferents," you just need some encouragement. You are where the majority of people find them-selves—in the middle.

Review your word associations on the quiz. For the most part, your words will describe special feelings about a color. For example, the usual reactions to blue include "calm," "peaceful," "cool," and "water." Blue sky tends to be pleasantly associated with clear days and the chance to enjoy being outdoors. It is the cool beauty of the reflection of sky on water, and the calm and constancy of the blue sky—although it may be dark and gloomy, we know that it's blue above the clouds.

Words associated with olive greens are usually grim rather than pleasant. Three frequent responses to this color are "army," "drab," and "sickness." The word "army" can be pleasant or unpleasant, depending on personal experience. But "drab" connotes colorless, dull, negative feelings, which are intensified by the word "sickness."

Pineapples In Your Past

At this point, you're not likely to know why you chose the words you did. Associations are not accidental—there is always an explanation. But your response is based on such "ancient history" that you can't remember its cause.

One of my clients told me that he couldn't stand anything pineapple yellow. He couldn't stand to look at it, smell it, and least of all, eat it. I was really intrigued by this violent aversion and asked him to try to recall the event that caused his reaction.

Since he couldn't think of any reason for it, he asked his brother if he remembered anything that might have happened when they were children. His brother reminded him that as children they had each snitched 25¢ from their mother's purse and splurged on pineapple sundaes. (Were sundaes ever really 25¢?) His brother also remembered that he had not only finished his own sundae, but went on to polish off the rest of his brother's.

Mother discovered the theft when they got home, but there was no need to punish them because they punished themselves by getting good and sick. The experience was only mildly traumatic, but it was enough to manifest itself in a long-term reaction to the color involved. The incident illustrates how we can spend the better part of our adult lives depriving ourselves of a particular color even though the reason has been lost to memory. Do you have any pineapples in your past?

Many people have associated olive toned-greens with childhood illness. Biliousness and nausea are associated with yellowish greens, and we are said to "turn green" when we are ill. Children are apt to associate illness with isolation, deprivation, and yucky medicines— enough to turn them off to olive-greens for years, if not forever.

When you recall an incident that provoked a negative reaction, you can often begin to overcome your prejudice by recalling a balancing positive aspect. When my client who hated lavender recalled the pain of her grandmother's funeral, she also uncovered precious memories that had been swept out of her mind by the trauma of the event.

A little "guided imagery" can help to overcome color negativism. I suggested that my client with the pineapple in his past imagine himself on a beach in Hawaii with the ocean on one side and luxuriant pineapple fields on the other. He then suggested the addition of a lovely dark-haired Hawaiian lady with a tray of Mai-Tais. Your fantasies can take you, too, to wondrous places!

Some of your own answers may surprise you by being unpredictable, even bizarre. When I took the word association quiz, I wrote "kindergarten" and "smiles" next to royal blue. It seemed like a strange combination until I remembered that my kindergarten teacher, Mrs. Phillips, always wore royal blue—with hair dyed to match. It brought back wonderful memories of a sweet person with a ready smile, the kind of teacher every child should have. Royal blue will always smile at me.

Celebrity Choices

Actor **Robby Benson** is attracted to anything that is red: food, packaging, cars, etc. He says that in a store, he's a sucker for red. In spite of the fact that he strongly favors the PM colors, orange turns him off. Robby told me, "When I was a child, it seemed all medicines came in the most vibrant oranges and because of those memories, I dislike that color the most."

But there are lots of other colors he associates with good thoughts. Peach, soft pink, and brown are "Karla's cheek, Karla's love, and Karla's eyes." Karla is his lovely wife and they are newlyweds! Vivid pink is winning at the races (the jockey's shirt), Forest Green is fairy tales, and sky blue means eternity.

He likes to wear blue, a wonderful choice for his Sunset blue eyes and his good thoughts about blue.

Melissa Manchester associates "Hawaiian sky" with royal blue. Tropical skies can indeed be incredibly blue. Melissa's color preference quiz found her almost equally divided between the Sunlight (Midday) and Sunset (PM) palettes, with Midday having a slight edge.

I see her surrounded by the soft shades of Midday during her "off-duty" hours but wearing the fiery sunset hues when she performs.

Ruth Manchester, Melissa's mother, is a designer who has worked with fabrics, and her answers were very texture-oriented. Peach is "silk" to her. You may also tend to think of color in terms of texture, especially if you are a touchy-type person. Are you one of those people who has to reach out and touch the fabric? It's just not enough for you to look at it? If so, you're lucky—you have another dimension to add to your enjoyment of beauty.

"Like mother, like daughter" has little relevance when it comes to color preferences. Ruth's associations were very different from Melissa's. Her personal preference was for the Sunrise palette, but as a designer, she has learned to work equally well with all of the palettes.

Melissa Gilbert, the lovely young woman we watched growing up on "Little House On The Prairie," wrote, "my high school gym shorts" next to royal blue. She checked the unpleasant column for that one—which tells us how she felt about her high school gym classes!

She chose the PM palette on her color preference quiz, with the Midday a close second choice. She wrote "my entire wardrobe" next to rust on the color association quiz, and indicated peach as "my room color." My advice to her is to continue to dress in the PM palette, because those shades are so becoming to her, but she could be content surrounding herself with colors from both Midday and PM palettes.

Telly Savalas has a strong affinity for Sunset colors. He sees color mainly as places and people. Olive is Greece (that's a good one!), aqua is the Mediterranean, and the Chamber of Commerce won't be thrilled to know that Los Angeles is grey. Bright green is St. Patrick's Day (as it is for many people), purple is Dracula, red is **Estee Lauder,** but peach is **Marilyn Monroe.** He sees some close friends as colors, but rust and brown, he says, are "Me."

A few years ago my family and I attended a weekend meeting at Rancho Bernardo, near San Diego. Soon after we arrived, my children wandered off, and I went looking for them. As I passed an open door in the hallway of the hotel, I looked inside.

There were ten kids of assorted ages, my own two included, sitting cross-legged on the floor around **Liza Minelli.** She invited me in, we discovered we were there for the same meeting, and we chatted—about color, of course.

I mentioned that whenever I had seen her perform, she almost always wore black and red, but at parties or premieres, she usually wore white. She replied that she loves the simplicity of black and white, but that red is, for her, the "kicker," signifying strength, excitement, and passion.

In her New York apartment, she has surrounded herself with the same starkly contrasting colors, accented by bold Andy Warhol paintings. Her bedroom has moire-covered walls and a tufted velvet headboard done in a vivid AM "Minelli red."

That was the weekend Liza fell in love with my son. At five years of age, however, he wasn't ready for a serious commitment.

The Enticing Rainbow

Compare your answers to those on the following list. These are the words most used to describe the colors in the quiz. Most colors have negative, as well as positive, connotations. As you will see, there are many more positive than negative associations.

For every negative response you had on the quiz, try to think of a balancing positive. The purpose of this quiz is to help you to rewind that wonderful tape recorder in your head so that you can reexamine your thoughts about color and open yourself up to that enticing rainbow.

Colors	Positive	Negative
Royal Blue	Flags, bright, kings, tropical ocean	Sharp
Navy	Uniforms, nautical, sea, conservative, service, sober	

Colors

Colors	Positive	Negative
Sky Blue	Heavenly, celestial, wet, cool, ice, peaceful	
Lavender	Delicate, nostalgia	Aging, insipid
Purple	Violets, royalty, mystical, artistic	Shadowy, mourning, melancholy
Yellow	Warm, friendly, radiant, sunshine, cheerful	Jaundice, cowardice
Orange	Glowing, bright, pumpkins, hot, harvest, juice, sunset	Too loud
Peach	Delicious, warm, inviting, ripe, fuzzy, juicy	
True Red	Hot, fire, intense, passion, energy, excitement, active	Rage, blood
Soft Pink	Feminine, icing, sweet, tender	Too sweet, cloying
Vivid Pink	Attention-getting, fun	Tacky, cheap
Wine	Rich, elegant, refined, tasty, velvet	
Brown	Earthy, dependable, secure, masculine	Dirty, soiled
Rust	Autumn, sunset	Rusty
Bright Green	Clear, moist, grass, St. Patrick's Day	Envy

Colors	Positive	Negative
Forest Green	Nature, cool, refreshing, restful	
Olive	Oil, army, tree	Drab, illness
Blue-Green	Ocean, clean, clear	
Aqua	Water, cool, refreshing, clean	Weak
White	Light, cool, clean, pure	Sterile
Black	Dark, night, sophisticated, sexy, dignified, serious	Mysterious, ominous, depressing, death
Grey	Flannel, neutral, rain, conservative, practical	Ghostly, somber, mousy
Beige	Warm, neutral, classic	Colorless
Taupe	Classic, neutral, practical	Colorless

The colors with the fewest negative connotations are usually sky blue, blue-green, forest green, navy, wine, and peach. This may be because of the positive thoughts they bring to mind: sky, ocean, forest, an alluring drink, a delicious fruit.

If your responses are very unlike those indicated, you are not strange—just different. And it is these differences that give us our individuality.

Most people discover that most of their favorable associations are in their preferred colortime palette. Chances are your least favorable associations will also be in your least favored colortime.

The purpose of these color exercises is to get you to analyze your responses, get rid of old prejudices, and open your mind to new color possibilities. If, however, you continue to detest a color (even though it's in your colortime), do not use it. It may simply be too difficult to deal with and there are many other shades and tints for you to use. If you suffer from color deprivation, it's not terminal—just tiresome!

The Color Clones:

Are Your Choices Influenced By The Colors Currently "In Fashion?"

When a color story is new and popular, the market is often inundated with it, either alone or in combination with another "now" color. About 20 years ago, powder blue and olive green were worn together for the first time. I can remember going to my first "Hollywood" party and feeling terribly unique and daring in that combination, only to find that the other five women present were wearing the identical colors!

High fashion colors can be exciting and novel, but become passé very quickly. Color trends can lead to color trouble. There is always a place for newness, but it should be used with caution. Bathrooms and bedrooms are good places for trendy colors since it is less expensive to change towels, bathroom carpets, and bedspreads than it is to redo an entire living/dining/family room area. Accessories, in interiors, clothing, personal stationery, table settings, linens, floral arrangements, and even in lighting, also provide relatively inexpensive opportunities to experiment with unique color combinations.

Color combinations often reflect historical periods and social trends, such as the "psychedelics" of the 60's. The emergence of the "hippie" counter-culture, political rebellion, dissonant rock music, the Beatles, pop art, and changing lifestyles found reflection in the bright oranges, luminous pinks, and neon greens used together during the period. But that kind of look can become tacky and dated very quickly.

Remember, you can only tolerate such screaming combinations for a short time.

It is fun to experiment with "new" colors, especially those to which you reacted very favorably on the association quiz. They are emotionally stimulating and novelty is intriguing. Are you ready for change? If the answer is a resounding "Yes"—now is the time.

Familiar colors give you a feeling of comfort and security. You may want to stay with colors that are old friends. But don't just stay with them out of habit—do it because it feels right. Color choices are often made because of peer and social pressure. If you make choices because of what is "socially acceptable" in your community, you can become a color clone whose house is either a boring replica of every other house on the block, or whose apartment looks like every other one in the building.

Murky Purple and Orange Lifesavers:

Do Other People Influence Your Choice of Color?

Do you allow other people to make your color choices for you? Is it because you lack the confidence to make your own choices? It is often easier to defer to another person's judgment (and also avoid responsibility for the wrong choices).

We often seek color opinions from other people, especially those whose taste we admire. There is nothing wrong with that, provided the other person is qualified to give advice. When you get unsolicited opinions, always consider the source. Remember, there are virtually no "rights," or "wrongs." It is simply a matter of how you choose to express yourself.

The guidelines and "how to's" of combinations in this book are designed to give you greater confidence. If you stifle your creativity and basic feelings about color, you will eventually regret it. If you chose a living room sofa because your daughter/husband/wife/mother-in-law/roommate/friend told you that it was the color you should have rather than because you liked it, you may regret not following your own instincts. You're also likely to end up resenting the advice-giver.

It is possible for two people who live in the same place and have very different color associations to find a happy compromise. A solution might be to use individual favorites in special places in the house, so that everyone may experience his or her favorites in a special den, library, workshop, sewing room, or whatever. I recently made that suggestion to **Jack Smith,** a columnist for the *Los Angeles Times.* He had written that his wife had chosen a deep purple carpet for their bedroom. He associated deep purple with melancholy and despair (funeral homes again?) and noted that he would prefer orange.

He quoted me extensively in the article, pointing out that I had said, "You are heading for trouble if you insist on exchanging purple for orange, especially if she is not ready for that change. Why don't you compromise by using orange in another area of the house where you spend a great deal of time—perhaps the garage?

He replied to that by saying "Whatever melancholy I experienced from walking over the purple carpet is neutralized, I suppose, by the bits of orange I have managed to scatter around the house, like emotional lifesavers. The bar stools, for example, have orange vinyl seats, and I have found that I can sit on one of those stools for a while, sipping a glass of champagne, perhaps, or chardonnay, and . . . the melancholy of the purple carpet goes away. Also, the cushions of our dining room chairs are orange—the same color as the stools, so actually my taste is well represented in the house, and my emotional needs are not irretrievably swallowed up in the murk of the purple carpet. Fortunately my wife likes orange, too; or at least she had the good grace to tolerate it for my sake. In fact, the carpet in her workroom is orange (or maybe persimmon), which explains, perhaps, why she often hums while she's ironing my shirts. If it made her happy, I'd paint the whole house purple . . . of course, I'd have to build a room over the garage for myself!"

You can tell that these two people are especially agreeable when it comes to each other's tastes. A woman who hums while she is ironing shirts and a man who would paint his house purple to please his wife just have to be special.

Red Lights and Scarlet Women

In What Cities or Countries Did You Spend Your Childhood?

Were you raised in an area where rigid rules, traditions, or social pressures governed the use of colors? The longer you live in an area, the more entrenched these same attitudes become. It takes a strong will or a rebellious nature to defy tradition.

Marilyn R., one of my most vivacious clients, surprised me by saying that she never used lively colors, especially the slightest touch of red. In her home town, the "bad girls" wore red, and lived in "houses" with red carpets, ret velvet draperies, and red lights. Her mother warned her that if she used red she might be mistaken for one of the "scarlet women" and "what would the neighbors say?!" So she avoided what she referred to as "street-walker red."

She was so sensitive to red that she was having trouble with the fact that her teenaged daughter wanted a red bedspread. Isn't it interesting how history repeats itself? Marilyn's mother had forbidden her to use red, and here was Marilyn balking at her daughter's wanting to use the color. The nosy neighbors of her childhood were long gone, and she had moved to another part of the country, but the old way of thinking persisted.

Her husband had wanted a red car for years, and she balked at that, too. After she took the Color Profile and we discussed how limited and dull her choices were, she decided to climb out of her rut. She is now racing around town in a little red car. She's allowing the yang red part of her personality to shine through.

Macho Man
What Area of the World Do Your Parents Come From?

This is an important question because color prejudices—no matter how unrealistic—can be handed down from one generation to another. Many people still associate "nostalgia," "delicacy," and "little old ladies" with lavender. Do they really associate the color with old age, or do they write it down because it was an automatic response learned long ago?

Steve M. told me he would never wear lavender. In his culture, it was the color of genteel older women. How could he, a macho man, relinquish his masculinity to lavender?

Years ago, there really were lots of little old ladies with sprigs of lavender at the throat and hair of a matching hue, but today grandma is more apt to be jogging around in pink sneakers and a lavender warm-up suit. Many men have gone beyond associating delicacy with pink and lavender and use both colors for button-down shirts and emblem T-shirts, with terrific results. But I'm afraid Steve won't be one of them. He's too hung up on lavender's association with old lace.

In my experience, women are more likely than men to have pleasant color associations, and men are more apt to be indifferent to many colors. It could be that little girls have traditionally been encouraged to spend docile playtimes with coloring books, whereas boys are spurred on to active pursuits. Little girls are also apt to shop with Mommy, watch her make color choices, and use her as a role model.

If you are a man with numerous pleasant color associations, you have probably developed an "eye" for color. It will be interesting to see how many more men develop this "eye" as men's and women's traditional roles continue to change.

Tradition

Our color choices are often influenced by the regions of our ancestors and the color traditions passed on to us through generations. For example, people who have rural European backgrounds often prefer pure, bright colors, while those from urban areas tend to like the neutral, delicate hues. Dark colors are chosen both for practical purposes and for the air of sophistication associated with them.

Regardless of where we live, we often choose colors to decorate our environments that are close to the temperature of our atmosphere.

Those from Latin backgrounds frequently choose warm colors, while Scandinavians prefer the blue of the cool waters surrounding their countries. The English often favor cool colors. Those who dwell in the tropics and in Africa traditionally choose the pure, bright warm hues associated with warm climates.

In the United States, warm colors are generally preferred in the West and Southwest, and cool colors in the Northwest, Midwest, and East. Most Americans still cling to the traditional use of deep or neutral tones in the winter, with bright colors emerging in spring. Brighter, happier colors appear in summer and harvest tones take over in the fall.

Unfortunately for those who like to wear their favorite colors year round, apparel departments tend to switch colors with the seasons— often very abruptly—and it can be difficult to shop for "your" colors at "their" time of year.

Nearby surroundings affect our preferences, too. Blue-green is often chosen by those living near water; if they also live in the tropical sunshine, they add greens, yellows, and oranges to their lists of favorites.

The symbolic relationship of blue is preferred by many Americans and Europeans. Many in the upper socioeconomic classes consider neutral, dark, and subtle colors to be the most tasteful; bright colors tend to be reserved for special occasions or trips to the tropics.

Among those of at least one culture, blue is verboten. The Yezidis of Armenia curse their enemies by saying, "May you die in blue garments!" Yet in much of the world, blue symbolizes fair skies, constancy, and love.

For Russians, the same word means both "beautiful" and "red." The red flag stands for social order. Cultivated Europeans in other countries often consider bright red vulgar. In the Orient, red is the runaway favorite. To the Hindus, red symbolizes life and joy.

In China and Bolivia, red is worn by wedding parties and guests to denote joy and love.

In the West Indies, Madagascar, and Bali death means departing for a better place, so cheerful colors are worn. Black remains a traditional mourning color in most cultures, as does purple.

In many cultures, brides have for centuries symbolized purity and innocence by wearing white, a tradition begun by the ancient Greeks. Greek brides, however, went a step further by painting their entire bodies white, and wearing white flowers in their hair. In England, brides wore green gowns to signify new life and fertility until Elizabethan times. In Western civilization, white stands for cleanliness and purity and is considered the opposite of black. In mainland China, white is the symbol of mourning. To the West African, white stands for the spirit of his dead ancestors, and is used at confirmation ceremonies.

When you move from one area to another, you may or may not shed your traditions. Some people stay with the old habits and others move on to experiment with the new.

The conservative type will wear a splashy print shirt in Oahu—but never in Ohio! There is always the question of appropriateness. That Hawaiian shirt might be just right at a luau but grossly out of place in a business meeting.

In many areas of the world, clothing is looked upon as an expression of creativity rather than as simply suitable covering for the body. As world travel, television, and motion pictures lower traditional barriers, people are using colors in more interesting and creative ways. But let's hope that we never reach the point where everyone looks the same the world over!

Many color associations are rooted in religion or mystic symbolism, others derive from the primitive responses to color of the earliest members of humankind.

Symbolism

Despite cultural differences, and regardless of origin, there are basic similarities in symbolism.

Primitive people were first influenced by the colors of day and night and the elements of their environment. The dark blue of night brought quiet and rest. On moonless nights there was total darkness. Darkness concealed danger, and superstition created evil forces bringing fear of the unknown, mystery, and foreboding.

The true blue of the daylight sky on a good day is associated with the coming of another day—dependable and consoling. Survival was difficult in primitive times, and a new day with any shade of blue was probably comforting. Even a grey sky could be a happy sight. Grey has long been associated with dependability.

Coolness is associated with heights and the upper atmosphere. The surface of water reflects the image of sky and deep clear water appears blue-green. Bodies of water are cool or cold—another blue association. Deep ocean blue is the color of silence. Clear blue sky is untroubled and serene. Deep blue-violets, navy, and almost-black midnight blue have many of the same associations as black.

The yellow of sunlight not only brought stimulation and activity, but warmth and light. Because the sun was all things to primitive people—the force that controlled life—it became the symbol of good.

The aggressive activities of hunting and conquest were always associated with red—the color of blood and fire. Green was and still is eternal, life-giving Nature—food, foliage, and shelter. The fresh green of spring means the awakening of life and connotes youth and newness. Even now, red is "stop" and green is "go."

Certain color associations stem from society's use of that color. We expect the bright reds of the stop sign, the fire engine, and the traffic light to warn of danger.

White has traditionally signified hospitals, doctors and nurses, but this association is beginning to wane. Many of our old stereotypes are changing, along with the colors. Although linen sales are still "white sales," it's now a real challenge to find a white sheet at a white sale.

Religion and Color

In Kabalism, an ancient form of Judaism, color symbolism was significant. Colors carried many of the same meanings to Egyptians, Babylonians, Assyrians, Greeks, Shintoists, Confucianists, Persians, and Druids.

The concentration of divine light was white. Black was understanding, because it absorbed all light. This may be a clue to the connection between black and sophistication since to be sophisticated is to be wise through experience.

Wisdom was grey—a combination of white and black. Mercy was blue, strength was red, and beauty was yellow.

Victory was green, signifying the combination of mercy (blue) and beauty (yellow). Glory was orange, combining strength (red) and beauty (yellow). Strength (red) and mercy (blue) led to the foundation of purple—the basis of all that is.

In the color symbolism of early Christianity, the Heavenly Trinity was blue for God the Father, yellow for God the Son, and red for God the Holy Ghost. Heaven was blue, earth was yellow, and hell, red. Green was Mother Nature—everlasting and faithful. Red was martyrdom and symbolic of the blood of Christ, and gold and yellow were power, glory, and splendor.

Blue was hope, peace, sincerity, and serenity. The Virgin Mary was often pictured in blue. Purple was endurance, penitence, and suffering. Many orders of nuns wore purple, as did martyrs. Rosaries often contain amethyst stones. White was chastity, simplicity, and purity. Nuns were married to the church in white. Black represented death and regeneration.

Many of these ancient meanings are still attributed to colors. They are passed on from generation to generation. Certain meanings seem contradictory. For example, black is associated with death, but also with sophistication. Yet the meanings remain similar in that black is seen as mysterious—whether the eternal mystery of death or the mystery of the sophisticated woman in black.

Psychological associations also hold sway—to one person, black is funerals, but to another, black is the smartly dressed aunt who brought exciting presents when she came to visit.

The Language of Color

Color associations have long flavored our use of language. These, too, are often contradictory.

For example, although yellow is sunshine and happiness, heathens were once marked in yellow, which was also the color of Judas' robe. The cowardly are thus either "yellow dogs" or just plain "yellow." They also have "yellow streaks" down their backs or "yellow bellies" on their fronts!

In the middle ages, jade was ground into powder and brought from the Orient to Europe. It was believed to have mysterious and occult powers, especially when used by jealous lovers to gain the attention of the objects of their affections. Hence "green-eyed monsters" who turned "green with envy."

Young plants are green, so when you are inexperienced, you are also "green." If you have good luck growing things, your thumb is "green." And because our dollars are printed in that color, they are called "greenbacks."

Sometimes the connection is much more direct. If we party too much we're apt to become "green around the gills"—just as a sick fish does!

Red is the most passionate of all colors because of its earliest associations with blood and fire. Red associations are never timid, and often express opposite passions. Love is the red heart of Valentine's Day, but we also "see red" when we're very angry or hate something.

When we are broke, we are "in the red"—the bookkeeper uses that color to give us the bad news—because we may not have a "red cent to our names." When we want to have a good time, we "paint the town red," and special days are "red letter days."

We get entangled in "red tape," and a red light in the window may mean a scarlet woman in the house!

Pink is far less passionate because it is a watered-down red. So when we are pleased, but not necessarily ecstatic, we are "tickled pink." (It could also mean that we turn pink when we are tickled.) When we're happy, we look at the world through "rose-colored glasses" and when we're healthy, we're "in the pink."

Blue has a multitude of meanings. The nearer it is to black, the darker the associations. For example, we are "blue" when we are depressed, and we sing the "blues." We go back to school or work on "blue Monday." When blue is as constant as the daylight sky, the associations are much happier. So we have "true blue" friends and a constant stream of talk is a "blue streak."

The blue worn by the bride, as in "something old, something new, something borrowed, something blue," symbolizes fair skies and everlasting love.

"Blue laws" are those that reflect the extremely Puritanical code of laws; the original laws were termed "blue" simply because the bindings of the book were blue. A "blue-blood" is said to hail from a noble or aristocratic family who would not tolerate ordinary red blood like that of the masses!

"Purple" is something we get with rage, because our complexions seem to take on that shade when we are boiling mad. Or we may be "born to the purple"—a term designating regal birth, majesty, power, and glory that derives from the wearing of purple by Roman emperors. Cardinals of the Catholic Church also wore purple, adding to the association of dignity with purple.

Lavender is linked with delicacy and romance (because of the undertone of pink, which is femininity). "Lavender and Old Lace" is a famous play about two dotty old ladies with a penchant for lacing certain guests' tea with a smidgin of arsenic. Lavender has become associated with age and nostalgia.

Violet is a moody color often associated with mourning and depression. In **Shakespeare's** play of the same name, Hamlet states: "I would give you some violets but they all withered when my father died."

Black is used frequently as a descriptive term. The association is often negative—we are in "black despair" or we give "black looks." The "black sheep" is an oddball—often in disgrace because he is so different from the rest of the family.

We "blackball" a person by putting him on a "blacklist." And if we "blackmail" him, we will both be in trouble. But there is a good side to black—that same bookkeeper who put is "in the red" can switch inks to put us "in the black."

White is purity, and also makes peace. So we "wave a white flag" to surrender or we "whitewash" our mistakes. And if the whitewash doesn't work, we cover it up by telling a "little white lie!"

Living Out Your Fantasies

Fran J. came to me to have her colors done. We discovered that her colortime was the Sunlight (Midday) palette. The sunshiny, subtle colors really did please her, and that's what she wanted her house to look like.

She wanted to redo the house, but her financial situation was extremely limited.

It was in dire need of redoing, but as a divorcee with two young children to raise, redecorating was not her number one priority. Still, it was so depressing to come home to a place that was shabby and colorless. Could she buy paint and/or wallpaper for her living room, kitchen, entryway, and family room, cover the two sofas, and tile the kitchen floor, for less than $1,500?

I told her that no decorating project is impossible if you're willing to do most of the work yourself. She does sew, and that was a help. I gave her the same advice I give to you—color is the key. When you know your colortime palette, you decide on the mood you want to convey, and choose the colors from within that palette to get the mood across. She was such a definite Midday person that the choice was easy.

I asked her a very important question, which I will also ask you. What is your fantasy of the environment you want to create? Do you have a picture in the back (or front) of your mind that is your dream? Hold on to that dream. If it is really what you want, you can have it. You may not be able to do it as expensively as you would like, but you can capture the mood.

Have you squirreled away pictures from decorating magazines for years, with an "Oh well, someday?" (I do the same thing with recipes—cut them out and never use them.) Just after you finish this book you can start your "someday"—even on a shoestring budget.

So I sent Fran off to the paint store, armed with her colortime swatches. At this point, a lot of my clients will say in a tremulous voice, "Aren't you going to go with me?" (with nervous anxiety exuding from every pore). If you have your swatches, you really don't need me.

She brought back a selection of paint chips. She chose only those colors she really liked. We talked about her personal associations with the colors she chose, and her fantasies. She wanted the house to be light, airy, restful, but with warmth. Nothing too serious—a house to live in, with a touch of whimsy. Most of all, Fran wanted her home to be pleasing to look at and enjoy.

Alive
With Color

183

The two most important colors she chose were a soft, slightly dusty rose and a Limoges blue. We used variations of these colors, plus neutrals and off-white accents, for various patterns and trim work in the four areas, being sure that each shade was in tune with the mood she was after.

At this point, she is still working on the house. She's doing it all herself and feeling so much better about the place. It has improved her mental attitude, as she puts it, and it's a joy to come home to. It is laborious, but it truly is a labor of love. And it can be for you, too.

John Ruskin, the late writer-critic, once said, "The purest and most thoughtful minds are those which love colour the most." Let's move on to the next chapter and give your pure and thoughtful mind some intriguing color insights to think about.

Chapter 6

Special Effects

Positives and Negatives

I had an interesting experience several years ago that taught me a great deal about color. Little fingers love to investigate knobs and locks and as a result, when my children were quite small, we all got locked into my bedroom closet together.

I tried to be brave, calm, and composed, but the children took one look at my face and panicked. It took fifteen minutes of yelling and banging on the door to finally rouse my husband who had been sitting on the patio happily enjoying his newspaper.

Five minutes after it happened, the children were off playing in the sandbox, but I was walking around in a slightly crazed condition with a very sore throat. Getting on an elevator was a real ordeal, and being in a plane wasn't too terrific either. Since my work involves traveling to conventions and meetings, my phobia was definitely hampering my life.

I knew that this closet experience probably related to some early childhood event that had really frightened me, but I could not remember what it was. I knew it wasn't darkness—which is frightening to many people—because the light had been on in the closet. I also knew that I needed a quick remedy to keep me from becoming completely unglued in an uncomfortable situation.

A friend told me about how hypnosis had helped her overcome anxiety. I was skeptical, since I associated hypnotism with altered states, trances, and show time. But I was curious, so I went to see **Arthur Ellen,** in Westwood, California, a marvelous man who has helped many people including famous athletes and performers, overcome phobias.

He asked me to describe the problem, which I did. He then asked me whether I visualized the experience in the closet in color or in black and white. I was amazed to realize that I saw it in black and white—imagine a color consultant thinking in black and white!

Arthur explained to me that most people see their problems in black and white. They often come in to him with a skeptical attitude, even though they say they want help.

Negative thoughts—the problems—are colorless. Positive thoughts—the solutions—are colorful. Black and white thinking places limitations on you. You can use color as a therapeutic tool to help free you from the problem by literally painting it away.

Replace the uncomfortable, bothersome, negative black and white picture with a colorful, comfortable, positive picture. In order for this experience to have any impact at all, you really have to concentrate on seeing and feeling the colors.

Imagine a place where you'd like to be, or recall a happy incident in your life. Put yourself in a peaceful garden, or walking on a deserted beach. Think of your favorite colors and your favorite colortime. It doesn't make any difference where you are—at work, in your car, or on an elevator. Ideally, you would be lying down at home, but your imagination is always with you.

The shades I chose were from my Sunset colortime. I visualized a magnificent sunset I had once seen in Acapulco. I watched the golden ball disappear into the hot purples of the distant sky, revelled in the dusky blues and the deep teal ocean.

I bathed in the silence and the dazzling beauty. I breathed deeply and relaxed. I remembered another description of a beautiful Baja California sunset as related by Jack Smith:..."the sky turned the color of pale sherry...the day's last light was like tarnished silver on the bay."

My anxiety was replaced with a sense of deep relaxation and peace. Every time I find myself in a situation where I am a little concerned about feeling claustrophobic, I paint a gorgeous sunset in my mind. Underground caverns and submarine rides are still not my idea of how to spend a fun day, but whenever I need a booster shot, I think in technicolor.

My personal experience with the power of suggestion made me a believer. I am not suggesting it as a panacea for all ills, but it is certainly worth a try. It won't cost you anything other than a moment of your time.

Therapist **David Poole,** of Santa Fe, New Mexico, also uses color to eliminate negative thoughts through neurolinguistic programming. He tells me that he asks his clients to substitute a favorite color for a negative word. Again, it's the concept of overcoming an unpleasant association by visualizing color.

Your Color Crutch

Dr. Beverly Block, an Encino, California psychotherapist, uses color with hypnotism as a therapeutic technique. She feels that you can calm or soothe yourself, diminish anxiety, and reduce stress through suggestion.

A crutch to lean on may get you over your stressful situation, whatever it may be. Why not a color crutch?

Dr. Block points out that we are highly suggestible. The power of suggestion is used successfully and often very skillfully in television commercials. For example, you may not be hungry, but an enticing eclair appears, oozing creamy custard, dripping luscious chocolate.

Suddenly, you're dying for an eclair—in spite of the fact that you're not really hungry!

Dr. Block often uses audio tapes to help her clients visualize color. She suggests certain colors and then invites you to experience them. This is especially helpful for people whose imagination needs a nudge.

Dr. Block and I have taught many seminars together, and it always delights us to see how people can change the quality of their lives—if they believe they can. I hope you believe you can. In our busy, stressful lives, it is not only important to take the time to stop and smell the flowers, it's important to take a good, long look at them.

Body Rhythms

You not only have your own special time slot in Nature's Color Clock, you also have an internal clock, called your body rhythm. You will feel and look better when you are in harmony with your colortime. The Color Clock can also help you to be in tune with the rhythms of your body.

In her book, *Biological Rhythms in Psychiatry and Medicine*, author **Gay Gaer Luce** tells us that people have always timed their actions by natural light and the environment. **Carl Linnaeus,** a Swedish naturalist, noticed that flowers opened and closed at different hours. Formal gardens were often planted to form a clock face and on a sunny day, the flowers could "tell the time" to within a half hour.

We are very much like flowers that open and close at different hours. Ms. Luce says that "We are calibrated to the rhythms of nature partly because of the senses we know, and perhaps also by the senses we only suspect to exist. One of the most important cosmic forces in our existence is sunlight, which may tune us to the rhythm of our planet."

She feels that people may be very much like the plant that only flowers if given the right amount of light.

Are You A Lark, A Robin, Or An Owl?

Which of the following statements fits you best?

1. My energy level is highest in the morning.

2. I really don't start to perk until my mid-morning coffee (tea) break.

3. My energy level goes up as the sun goes down.

In the morning, do you leap out of bed in a single bound, ready to attack the day? Maybe you're not quite that energetic, but if you are most alive in the morning, you have lots of company. You're a lark.

Do you stagger around in the morning hoping that someone points you in the right direction? Perhaps you're not stumbling into walls, but if your energy level has to wait for you to take flight somewhere around mid-morning, you're a robin.

Are you the late bloomer who blossoms later in the day? Are you finally ready to start working in the afternoon? While everyone else is nodding off at a party, are you still dancing (often by yourself)? You're obviously an owl.

Are you one of those rare individuals who would prefer to go all night and sleep all day? You are definitely in the minority. I can't resist calling you a bat (what else flies by night?). Your body rhythms may simply be different than most and you're happiest on a reverse schedule, or you have adjusted your life style to your odd hours. But if your favorite colors are mystery black and blood red, don't call me, I'll call you.

Your body temperature is related to your performance. Body temperature usually falls during the night, rises in the morning, and reaches a plateau sometime during the day. Your energy level rises with your temperature. The differences are very slight and patterns vary in individuals. They are also affected by illness.

You could chart your temperature patterns, but you really don't have to. You know your highs and lows.

We've all had to change our natural patterns to accommodate a partner or a job. Our school systems and workdays are designed for larks. Are you an owl, living with a lark? (Good luck.) Are you the mother lark who has to push her unconscious teen-aged robin out of the nest? It's really tough for a lark and a robin to share a nest. And if an owl invades your territory, watch out.

Most industrial accidents occur at 3 a.m., which is, for most people, an energy-low time. This is the hour of high errors and low efficiency. Airline pilots tested in Germany found that their mental performance reached a peak between 2 p.m. and 4 p.m. Their reaction times and psychomotor functions were best then, too. The worst responses occurred between 2 a.m. and 6 a.m.

Think of the possibilities for utilizing color visualization techniques in industry to increase production and decrease accidents. A quick shot of visualizing a high energy colortime could be a great way to get the adrenalin going.

Raising Your Energy Level

At what time of day do you feel most alive and energetic? If you are feeling tired and need a little push, take a moment to visualize the colors in your high-energy colortime. If you chose morning as your vital time of day, visualize the AM colortime, especially the vibrant reds and yellows. Concentrate on your high-energy colortime when you need a lift. You can also use a photograph, a painting, or a poster to focus on.

I do my writing in the bedroom. I have a **Jacques LaLande** poster of three children walking across a meadow with the sunlight behind them. Whenever I need a quick shot of energy, I look up at the poster and imagine myself in that scene. I have a thing for meadows—especially in the middle of the day. Midday is my high-energy colortime.

Relaxation and Relieving Tension

In which time period are you most relaxed?

> **1.** In the early part of the day.
>
> **2.** Around lunchtime, in the middle of the day.
>
> **3.** In the afternoon and evening.

There is a state of relaxation that occurs in everyone, at various times of the day, called the alpha state or alpha rhythm. In laboratory testing, many people have been able to control or sustain this alpha rhythm by imagining scenes and using other visual images.

In the book *Insomnia*, authors **Gay Gaer Luce** and **Dr. Julius Segal** explain that learning to control the alpha state through meditation and yoga helps to combat tension and psychosomatic illnesses, and can help you to achieve a plateau of serenity.

They contend that everyone experiences alpha states and can learn to induce them. You can sit quietly in a room "with your eyes fixed upon a particular point, while concentrating on a favorite fantasy until the world fades away and you feel relaxed and detached from the room and its noises."

They feel that it could take ten minutes to relax sufficiently but if you focus on some point in the room, "other thoughts and the world around you will no longer interrupt."

The authors suggest doing the following popular yoga exercise:

> **1.** Lie flat on your back, relaxing as completely as possible.
>
> **2.** Imagine your consciousness at the tip of your toes.
>
> **3.** Slowly start to draw your consciousness smoothly through your body, beginning with the toes, ankles, legs, arms and neck.

Alive
With Color

4. Relax the muscles of each area as you slowly draw your consciousness up into your head.

5. You should now be totally relaxed and be able to concentrate on an inward image of a deep blue light. Continue to concentrate on that light for three minutes for maximum relaxation.

I am sure that blue was chosen because it suggests peace and calm. Many of my clients find it more helpful to concentrate on a total image than on a single color.

My favorite aunt, a lady of 70-plus, is a mountain hiker, a dancer, and a constant inspiration to me. She has been doing this yoga exercise for years, but she prefers to visualize scenes in the PM colortime because this is the time of day when she is normally most relaxed.

You may choose to focus on the colortime palette in which you feel most relaxed. For many people, this would be the PM colortime. If you are more relaxed in the early part of the day, visualize the AM colors.

One of my clients, **Liz P.,** is a teacher who keeps a travel poster on the wall of her classroom. The scene is a dewy, brilliantly green Irish countryside at sunrise. When her rambunctious four-year-old preschoolers start to get to her, she concentrates on the colors of the poster. It's better than a tranquilizer.

Are you most relaxed in the middle of the day? Imagine yourself bicycling along a country road until you find just the right spot to picnic in the sunshine. One of the nicest things about using your imagination is that you can become a kid again. You can play all you like. Forget about being a responsible adult for a while.

You can, of course, carry your relaxation to the ultimate degree and nod off. You can become so relaxed that you slip right off to sleep. Shirley, my dear assistant, can take cat-naps at will. She concentrates on her relaxing Midday palette and off she goes—anywhere and any time.

She even sleeps on the job, but I don't mind at all. She often waits (in the next room) for me to finish my lecture, which she has heard hundreds of times. It gives her a refreshing pick-me-up, and she returns ready to give the clients her full, wide-eyed attention.

I would suggest that you try it on your job, but I don't know how your boss would feel if he found you unconscious at your desk!

Everyone fantasizes. Call it daydreaming, call it wishful thinking. Call it anything you like, but see it in color. Think about the time of day when you do your best work. Think of that colortime when you need some cerebral stimulation. Create the scenario and then step into it, or keep a photo handy for inspiration.

If you have trouble recalling the shadings of a particular palette, simply look back at the colortime palettes. It is often difficult to see colors that are not in your preferred palette. You may practice "selective viewing," which means that when you walk into a store or other environment, you do your best to ignore the colors you do not like—you treat them as if they don't exist because they are so distasteful to you. Your eye searches for the colors you relate to best.

You may call yourself a "morning person" because that is when your energy level is at its highest and you are at your most productive, but you still may choose to decorate your home in the PM colortime because those colors appeal to you most. The colortime you visualize may not always coincide with the color you choose for your environment. You may not choose to wear or surround yourself with bright turquoise, but could you really dislike a tropical turquoise ocean? Choosing a scene from nature is the easiest way to visualize the desired color and keep it from offending your eye.

Lee Bergere, who plays the part of Joseph, the major domo on "Dynasty," says that he is most relaxed at Midday, but his least preferred colors, according to his Colortime Quiz, are the Midday colors. I would never suggest that he decorate with the Sunlight Midday palette, especially since his word association quiz told me that he doesn't relate to confection colors well. But I would suggest that he visualize the gentler Sunlight colors while he is taking a quick rest on the set.

There are warm colors as well as cool colors in every colortime. The cooler colors are tranquil, the warm colors are energizing. Always end your scenario with the color of the desired effect. If you are exercising and run out of steam, take a moment to visualize your high-energy colortime. If that is the AM colortime, and you have chosen a field of fresh flowers to visualize, draw your image to an end by focusing in on the cheerful yellow daffodils.

When I visualize my sunset scene, my eye lingers last and longest on the serenity of the dusky blue over a matching ocean.

The Color Clock gives you the freedom to use different palettes for different purposes. Instead of narrowing your choices, you can open yourself to experiencing more pleasure with color. The only limits you have are the limits of your own imagination.

Celebrity Couples

Actress **Nancy Olsen** suggested to me that it might be interesting to compare various couples' color preferences to see how similar or different they are. Do people of similar tastes find each other, or do opposites attract? I am happy to report that both are true, as far as color is concerned. Perhaps in a long-standing relationship, people may develop similar tastes, but those with differing tastes can also live happily ever after.

What I did find is that with most of the couples I queried, both often had the same body rhythm patterns. Larks do seem to be attracted to other larks, robins to robins, and owls to owls!

Nancy Olsen and her husband, entertainment executive **Alan Livingston,** have different tastes and feelings about color. Nancy prefers sundappled meadow scenes as a background and Alan prefers warm, earthy backgrounds (as many men do, especially in a den).

They have effectively compromised, and their lovely Beverly Hills home tastefully reflects their choice of palettes. They are both robins.

Jim Backus, the loveable nearsighted Mr. Magoo (as well as many other characters we all know) and his wife **Henny** might choose clothing colors in different palettes, but they both like Sunrise colors for decorating. They are two owls who found each other!

Dusty Baker, of the Los Angeles Dodgers, and his wife **Harriet** like both the Sunlight and Sunset colors for their environment. Dusty and Harriet are both owls. I suggested to Dusty that he think Sunset colors before coming to bat for a quick shot of energy! Dusty says that he does prefer night games to day games, which doesn't surprise me because of his body rhythm. He also says that he would prefer his uniform to be a more exciting Dodger Blue.

Mariette Hartley, the actress, and her husband, director **Patrick Boyriven,** are both robins. Mariette is a PM golden redhead with blue eyes. She looks wonderful in combinations of warm earthy tones, especially combined with the blues and blue-greens of her palette. Patrick uses the traditional crossover colors of navies and greys with touches of red or wine in his ties and breast pocket. But he is also an artist and this is where his love of color really breaks out. He and Mariette have used all three palettes to reflect different moods in various rooms in their home. Contrast is very important to him, especially in filmmaking.

Sherry Hackett, wife of comedian **Buddy Hackett,** associates color in combinations and variations. Every color leads her to another. On her Color Profile Quiz, she placed mauve next to peach. All of the bright colors were associated with something softer: light red next to true red, soft pink next to vivid, softer pink next to pink, lavender with purple, and beige with orange.

Evidently Sherry has always been tuned into color blending. When she cooked her first dinner for Buddy right after they were married, all of the food had to match! I have never really thought about mono-chromatic meals, but it might be fun to try, or at least consider the possibilities of food combinations. Their clothing color choices are different, but they both agree on the Sunset palette for interiors.

And then, of course, there's the handsome twosome of **Princess Diana** and **Prince Charles.** She is the perfect example of a Sunrise, light ash blonde with milk white skin. The Royal jewel colors are magnificent on her: sapphire, amethyst, aquamarine, and especially her favorite shade of emerald green. Prince Charles has that wonderful English skin that is beige tinged with a healthy ruddy glow. It's reported that his favorite kilt is a mixture of dove grey and melon—an attractive combination for his Midday colortime.

Physical Phenomena

Physiology is the branch of biology that deals with the functions and activities of life, and of the physical phenomena involved. Scientists have found that actual physiological changes take place in human beings and animals when they are exposed to certain colors.

As I have pointed out, colors can stimulate, excite, depress, soothe, and even tranquilize, so your state of mind, and your health, can be affected. Color is light and light is energy. Research proves that light and color can influence not only our moods, but our physical well-being.

Tests have shown that bright red or yellow drives up blood pressure and increases respiration and pulse rates. These colors also increase muscle tension and eye-blinking. Red is a stimulant that peps up the autonomic nervous system. We actually do feel warmer in a red room and cooler in a blue room. Experiments found that a female subject began to feel cold at 59 degrees fahrenheit in a blue-green room, but did not feel chilly in a red-orange room until the temperature fell to 52 degrees!

An executive for a paint company received complaints from workers in a blue office. They had to wear sweaters and constantly complained of the cold. The office was painted a warm peach. The sweaters came off, even though the temperature had not changed.

Color preferences are apt to change with the weather. If it is very hot (100 degrees), most people prefer cool blues. If the temperature is in the 60's, red is the first choice. If the temperature drops below freezing, red usually remains the first choice.

Visually, red expresses nearness and warmth; blues, distance and coolness. Warm colors advance, cool colors retreat. The eye actually sees more warm colors than it does cool. Light or bright colors expand size, deeper shades contract. Yellow is seen as the largest color, after which come white, red, green, blue, violet, and black.

As you might expect, the hottest colors are red-oranges and the coolest are blue and blue-violet.

The colors that gain our attention fastest are at the warm end of the spectrum—red, orange, yellow, yellow-green. Yellow and orange are the most visible colors, especially on a rainy day. Yellow stickers are thus not only cheerful, but practical, as are the orange vests of the highway workers.

White is seen as lighter in weight than black. **Bonnie Bender,** manager of the Color Marketing, Coatings and Resins Division of **PPG Industries,** described a study in which engineers experimented with boxes. They took several, in varying weights, and painted the heavy boxes white and the light-weight boxes black. Workmen had more trouble lifting the black boxes, which were lighter in weight, than the white boxes, which were actually heavier!

Length seems longer and weight seems heavier under a red light. Length is judged to be shorter and weight is judged to be lighter under a green light. The passage of time can be overestimated or under-estimated, depending on the color of a room. Time is perceived as moving more slowly in a red room and more quickly in a blue or green room.

The noted psychoneurologist, **Dr. Kurt Goldstein,** states that color stimulation is an important consideration for human beings. In his book, *The Organism*, he writes about a woman who often stumbled and walked unevenly. The color of her clothing had a definite effect on her awkwardness. When she wore red, she fell frequently, but when she wore green or blue, her balance was restored.

It seems that screening out the red light rays has a relaxing effect. Dr. Goldstein says that people suffering from muscular tension and twitching might find relief by wearing green glasses.

Yellow Houses Sell Best

The hues that we remember best are yellow, green, red, and white. This helps to explain why yellow houses sell best or have the most curb appeal, as they say in the real estate business. Not only are they memorable, they also connote instant warmth by being associated with sunshine. So if you want to sell your house, paint it yellow!

Some people can sense color by touch. A test was conducted by a psychology professor at Barnard College in New York on a woman who was found to have the ability to identify different colors on pieces of paper just by touching them.

As far as the psychologist could determine, the critical factor was heat. Black or dark shades absorb more heat than white or light colors, within a certain temperature range. The woman's fingertips were sensitive to the thermal variations and transmitted this information to the brain. Ordinary people must rely on the retinas in their eyes. According to experts, the amount of stimulation that a color causes in the retina translates directly into our emotional reaction to that color.

In another study, three women were given identical brands of detergent in three differently colored boxes. The first box was yellow, the second blue, and the last was yellow and blue. They tested the detergents and found that the one in the yellow box was too strong, the one in the blue box was too weak, and the one in the two-tone box was just right!

Colors are often used in placebos, inert medications (usually no more than a gelatin capsule) used for the mental relief of a patient rather than for their actual effect on the disorder. In a study done at a leading university, when subjects were asked to categorize the effects of pills (which were actually placebos) by their colors, reds and yellows were perceived as stimulants and blues as depressants.

Do You Smell Green?

The best-smelling colors are thought to be cool green, aqua, pink, warm yellow, and lilac. Our senses are all intertwined. Scents and colors are inevitably tied together. The perfume industry has used this fact to great advantage. You can often look at a bottle of perfume and sense how it will smell when you sniff it.

You can't help but associate a green cologne with freshness and nature, which is why so many aftershaves and astringents are cool greens and aqua. You expect that pink, rose, lavender, and lilac-colored toilet waters will smell light, delicate, and somewhat sweet.

The trend in the last several years had been to musky animal or exotic scents. These are almost invariably done in ambers and topaz, the colors of earthy spices and deep woods.

The color of the container may mask the color of the liquid, but the bottle color gives the message. You know that a perfume called "Red" has got to be exciting. A new perfume has been advertised as the "liquid expression of colorful sensuality...exploding with exotic florals...found in a forbidden garden...slightly dangerous, but worth the risk!" It is packaged in electric blue—the message is that you are super cool, but underneath there is smoldering warmth. The bottle is embellished with a gold snake for the male, and a snake of bright blue, green, and white, with touches of red and yellow, for the female; they are of course, intertwined.

The names of scents immediately conjure up color as well as scent to help get their messages across to you. For example:

Night—*Sophistication*
Cinnabar—*Oriental, spicy*
Violets, Lilac—*Flowery and feminine*
Blue Grass, Celadon, Fresh Lemon—*Clean, refreshing*
Tea Rose—*Delicate*
White Linen—*Crisp and summery*
White Shoulders—*Sexy, but ladylike*
White Lace—*Romantic*
Black Suede—*Handsome and smooth*
Ivoire—*Quiet sophistication.*
Grey Flannel—*Classic, correct*

Men's scents are never done in pinks and violets, which are considered too feminine. They are usually in woodsy or green shades, and occasionally in blue; these colors are thought to be more masculine.

Pink Cells

A great deal of publicity and attention has been given recently to the quieting effect of a bright color called Baker-Miller pink. **Alexander Schauss,** of the American Institute for Biosocial Research in Tacoma, Washington, developed the concept of using an intense pink for calming after he noted that his blood pressure, pulse, and heart beat lowered more rapidly after a period of hyperexcitement when he viewed that color.

He felt that it might have an effect on human aggression and tested the theory at the Naval Correctional Center in Seattle. An admission cell was painted the Baker-Miller pink.

New confinees were admitted to the cell and observed for 15 minutes during which no incidents of erratic behavior were recorded. The effects of the color lingered on for at least 30 minutes after their removal from the cell. The study has been repeated in several other facilities, with equal success.

Many people, including myself, were surprised to find that the pink used was rather bright—not at all docile. Some of my more skeptical colleagues felt that because pink is still pink after all—the color of valentines, love, and icing on the birthday cake—it follows that pink should subdue the subjects.

But how does this explain the fact that color-blind subjects at Bryce Hospital in Tuscaloosa exhibited the same physiological responses to Baker-Miller pink as those who were not color-blind?

Schauss states that "the effect of Baker-Miller pink is physical, not psychological or cultural." Although a person may not be able to differentiate color, transmitters in their eyes pick up information from visible radiant energy sources and transmit that energy to the hypothalamus, and the pineal and pituitary glands.

In other words, you may also "see" with your glands.

Blue Bedrooms and Blue Classrooms

Different values of pink, however, may have totally different effects. **John H. Ott,** in his book, *Health and Light,* tells the story of a radio station in Florida where the lighting was changed from regular white fluorescent tubes to a deep pink color. Everyone began to notice an air of disagreement and irritability as announcers failed to perform well and tempers flared.

Someone finally thought of the pink tubes and suggested removal. Within a week, the situation had improved.

Other members of the animal kingdom also have problems with deep pink. In the same book, Ott tells of experiments with minks to test their reactions to different colors of glass and plastic. Minks kept behind deep pink glass were extremely aggressive, if not downright nasty. They are not known for their charming personalities anyhow, but when they were placed behind blue plastic, they become docile and amiable.

An interesting P.S. to this story is that all of the females became pregnant after mating in the blue cages. You might want to think about that before you paint your bedroom blue!

In an article written for the *International Journal of Biosocial Research*, **Harry Wohlfarth** and **Catherine Sam** explain the effects of color and light in the environment on dependent handicapped children in an Edmonton, Canada school. The children often exhibited "unprovoked aggression, tantrums, a short attention span."

The study was done in three phases. In Phase I, orange, brown, and yellow were the main colors in the classroom. In Phase II, the main colors were variations of blue. In Phase III, the conditions were returned to the Phase I colors.

The Phase II colors, the blue environment, had the most favorable effect. The aggressive behavior lessened and the subjects had their lowest blood pressure readings. Interestingly, blind and sighted subjects were equally affected by the color changes.

Dr. Richard Kavner and **Lorraine Dusky,** in an interesting book titled *Total Vision*, tell of experiments in which the faces and necks of subjects were illuminated, but their eyes were tightly closed. They moved their arms toward a red light and away from a blue light. Blind people were observed to react the same way, which indicates "that color can affect us when absorbed through the skin."

Those who are totally blind often "see" color, especially as it relates to the other senses. **Helen Keller** wrote in *The World I Live In*, "I understand how scarlet can differ from crimson because I know that the smell of an orange is not the smell of a grapefruit . . . through an inner law of completeness, my thoughts are not permitted to remain colorless."

Stevie Wonder's lyrics are often quite visual. He "sees" color both in his songs and in the titles he gives them, like "Girl Blue," "Golden Lady," "Ebony Eyes," and "Black Orchid."

Humans can distinguish more than two million colors, shades, and tints, although only 7,000 have been named and classified. About one man in 12 and one woman in 200 have inherited defects in their retinas which result in color-blindness. Some color-blind people have been helped to discern color by wearing a pink contact lens in just one eye.

For many years it was thought that babies could not differentiate color, but recent tests show that infants can distinguish colors as soon as two or three months after birth. They are most attracted to pure, primary colors, such as red, blue, yellow rather than to blends of those colors. Gone are the days of namby-pamby nursery colors, but parents should avoid over-stimulating a child with too many bright colors.

I would not want to wake up in the middle of the night to see cookie monsters and fuzzy bright creatures with luminous glass eyes peeking out of every nook and cranny, so I often warn clients not to overdo a child's room.

The Birds and The Bees and Other Things

Even insects have color preferences. Mosquitoes are less apt to nibble on you when you are wearing yellow, orange, or white, but they love to munch on bodies in dark blue, dark red, and brown.

Flies are turned off by pale colors, especially blue. Barn stalls are often painted blue to keep the flies away. If you are really having a hard time with these pesky creatures, you might buy a pitcher plant. Its reds and yellows and aroma make it look—and smell—like rotting meat!

The unsuspecting fly slides down the slippery inner walls into the liquid at the bottom and drowns. Isn't that a lovely story? On second thought, you might just want to invest in a fly swatter.

Bees are attracted most to bright floral prints, especially with blue, yellow, or violet flowers. A flower called the mirror orchid attracts certain male wasps. The orchid looks incredibly like a female wasp in color, shape, and scent. Would you believe that the male wasp goes after the flower, not for the nectar or food, but because he is infatuated with it? In his ardor, the wasp picks up pollen from the orchid and deposits it on another female orchid. The moral of the story is "never trust a male wasp."

Since most insects are nearsighted, scent is what first attracts them to flowers, but many blossoms have colored "roadways" which lead the insect to the nectar.

Your pet turtle or snake has better color vision than your cat or dog. Dogs have very little color vision and cats can only see color on large surfaces. Birds are most attracted to red flowers and red fruits, but are partially blind to blue. And, as you might expect, rats are color-blind.

Fishes are ambivalent about red. They are either greatly attracted to it or avoid it totally. Deep-water fish often respond only to deep blue, and sharks are greatly attracted to the color that a marine biologist calls "Yum-Yum Yellow"!

Generally speaking, the more colorful the species, the better the color vision. So peacocks and parakeets probably see better color than mice and men!

Crafty Chameleons

We have long recognized the ability of animals to survive in their environment by taking on the color of their surroundings. The fawn disappears into the dappled sunshine of the woods wearing a matching coat. Jungle animals fade into their backgrounds, as do the crafty chameleons.

It took humans a while to learn to emulate chameleons. The red-coated British were prime targets against the terrain of India until someone thought to match their uniforms to the local mud tones. The

Indian word for mud is now known throughout of the world as "khaki."

Speaking of camouflage, on a segment of "M*A*S*H," **Clete Roberts** interviewed **Alan Alda** and asked him what he liked least about being stationed in Korea. Alda's reply was "green—green jeeps, green tents, and green uniforms." The only things that weren't green, Alda grumbled, were the vegetables.

From that same wonderful show, **Jamie Farr,** (Cpl. Klinger of Toledo, Ohio) has only one unpleasant association with any color and that's also with drab army green. He says after years of wearing it both for real and 11 years on M*A*S*H, he can do without it. As a matter of fact, on one segment of the show, he developed such an aversion to it that he broke out in hives wherever it touched his body. He had to wear a silk slip under his green uniform!

One shade of green from his PM palette that he really feels comfortable with is hunter green. It reminds him of the forest and Robin Hood, and he's surrounded himself with its natural verdant feeling in his home in a charming rustic area of the San Fernando Valley.

Health, Color, and Light

Color and light have been used to treat illness for centuries. Amulets, gemstones, insects (dead or alive), flowers, feathers, dyes—scores of natural objects and substances were thought to have special healing powers based on their color.

The color used to treat the illness was often the "color" of the illness itself. The three main colors used for treatment were red, green, and yellow.

Even in modern times, there are practitioners who use colored light as a curative. They believe that red light can be used to treat ailments such as low blood pressure, eczema, circulatory problems, and sore throats. Blue light is used to cure infections, headaches, and high blood pressure, and green is used for emotional disorders such as anxiety and for infections. Violet is thought to help insomnia, and yellow is believed by some to be a muscle stimulant and nerve builder.

Chromotherapists, as they are called, are looked upon with skepticism in this country, because they have been associated with quackery. However, there are some accepted forms of colored light treatment used by the medical profession today.

In an article called, "The Guiding Light," from *Psychology Today*, science writer **Hal Hellman** states, "Researchers are becoming convinced that all aspects of our health, mental as well as physical, are affected by the intensity, duration and even the color of the light to which we are exposed."

Hellman notes that animals (and people) have daily rhythms that are cued to the time of day and that sunlight affects various daily and seasonal activities. Farmers have been fooling chickens for a long time by keeping lights on in the hen house to extend the days in winter and thereby increase egg production. Having raised chickens at a particularly organic time in my life, let me tell you that it is not hard to fool a chicken! The hens respond to light energy entering the eyes and it stimulates their pituitary glands. Mr. Hellman reports in his article that **Dr. Alfred Lewy,** formerly of the National Institutes of Mental Health and now with the University of Oregon Health Sciences Center, is using broad-spectrum lighting to treat patients who become depressed in winter and recover in spring, and is working with other seasonal illnesses such as ulcers. His area of research is the response to light of the human hormonal system. Scientists believe that we will learn a great deal more about light—intensity, time of day applied, and color—that will be helpful to our health.

John Ott, one of the world's leading experts on lighting, has done years of research to help bring about full-spectrum fluorescent lighting that closely duplicates natural sunlight. He feels that light is a critical factor in our total environment, and that it has an important impact on our general health and well-being.

Sunlight has been used as a remedy for many illnesses. Lack of sunlight is a factor in the development of rickets, many bone disorders, and Vitamin D deficiencies. Sunlight draws many people like a magnet, perhaps because of the inherent need for it.

Another form of color and light that many find irresistible is fire. Some anthropologists believe that the reason many people are mesmerized by the flickering lights and color of the television set is because it is a throwback to the time when our earliest ancestors sat around watching the flickering lights and color of the fire!

School children in a full spectrum-lit classroom were found to have fewer cavities than those under cool-white light. Animal experiments showed similar results. No one knows exactly why but the answer may lie in the stimulation of hormones and other body chemicals by full-spectrum lighting.

Premature infants with jaundice are treated under blue lights that penetrate the skin. Ultra-violet lights are used to clean the air of operating rooms. Black light is used to treat psoriasis.

Doctors often diagnose diseases by color—the red eyes of the alcoholic, the yellow skin of jaundice, the blue skin of heart disease, and the black nails of fungus infection. They can even spot the orange skin of the chronic carrot-eater!

Sophisticated diagnostic tools are available through the infra-red thermograph, which can locate disease and injury with a scanning camera. Since each part of our body has a different temperature range, each is recorded as a color. When the thermograph records changes from the norm, the source of the problem can be pinpointed.

Laser beams, which are intense beams of light, are being used to burn tumors away, control bleeding in surgery, and fuse retinas to the back wall of the eye. Eventually they may be used to unclog fatty deposits in the arteries.

Auras

Numerous people over the centuries have claimed the ability to read "auras," the luminous radiation of colors that emanate from the body. Religious idols have often been depicted as possessing this divine light of energy.

Among those who claim to see auras, there are many interpretations of what color emanations mean, but when you are surrounded by an aura, the following messages and colors are generally linked:

Warm red—*Affectionate nature*
Deep red—*Anger, physical vitality*
Bright red—*Sexuality, courage, irritation, egotism*
Pink and rose—*Love of family and devotion*

Dull brown—*Penny-pinching, selfishness*
Brown-orange—*Lack of ambition, repression*
Grey—*Depression, fear, sorrow, grief*
Orange—*Pride, ambition, energy*
Red-orange—*Healing, vitalizing*

Yellow—*Intellectual, mental concentration*
Grey-green—*Deceitful and sly*
Bright green—*Ingenuity, abundance, healing*
Pale green—*Sympathy*
Dark blue—*Religious belief, integrity*

Royal blue—*Honesty, loyalty, deep involvement*
Light blue—*Noble ideas, devotion, healing love*
Black—*Hatred, evil, malice*

White—*Purifying, uplifting*
Pale yellow—*Sickness*
Red-purple—*Power of the body, worldly*
Violet—*Spiritual*

It is interesting to note that many of the meanings given to auras are similar to the associations you learned about in the last chapter, and the psychological meanings you will learn about in the following chapter. So many of our beliefs are rooted in religion and mysticism and then passed on from generation to generation.

Everyone is said to have a major aura color, which may fluctuate with your mood and state of health. Many clairvoyants, such as the late **Edgar Cayce,** are great believers in the human aura. **Linda Clark** states in her book, *The Ancient Art Of Color Therapy*, that Cayce saw auras and believed that a person's favorite color was his or her major aura color. In her case, he was right. She feels that many average people who see auras are interested in spiritual growth, regardless of their religion.

Since I am so interested in anything involving color, I had my aura "read." The woman who did the reading saw my favorite Sunset colortime shadings as my aura. I observed that she chose colors that matched the personal coloring of everyone in my group—which may or may not have been a coincidence.

In recent years, new credibility has been given to the existence of a human aura through a process called "Kirlian photography." This specialized kind of photograph records a halo emanating from the body by means of a powerful electric charge. Physical and emotional states may then be ascertained and treated.

You may or may not be a believer in things mystical, or in ESP, but I find it best to keep an open mind. Would our great-great-grand-parents have believed that living, talking images could be dancing around in a box in our homes? Our great-grandchildren will undoubtedly experience colorful phenomena that we can only imagine.

Grey Eggs and Turquoise Bread

Whether or not you realize it, you eat with your eyes. This was proven as part of a research experiment that took place at a large Canadian university. The menu was not unusual, but the food colors certainly were.

Purple tomato juice was followed by grey eggs served on turquoise bread, dark blue mashed potatoes, orange-yellow rolls, pale blue butter, and bright green mashed banana, with black custard for dessert.

Needless to say, nobody finished the meal and some felt sick. This was ordinary, wholesome food dyed with harmless, tasteless colorings. The unusual colors were the culprits that turned the diners off.

We are so conditioned to expecting foods to be certain colors that our brain finds it difficult, even impossible, to make the transition to an unexpected color.

In the early days of our marriage, my husband and I took turns making sumptuous breakfasts on Sunday morning. One week, he decided to add a touch of the exotic by scrambling the eggs with a little wine. Red wine is a blue-red and you know what happens when you add blue to yellow. My stomach did a slow turn as I looked down at the green eggs. They actually were delicious, but I had to eat them with my eyes closed!

Chickens that have been fed cottonseed meal produce eggs with greenish yolks that, although nutritionally equal to the usual yellow egg yolks, just aren't as acceptable. This is the result of cultural conditioning. In Britain, for example, brown eggshells are more popular than the white shells preferred in the United States.

Special
Effects

210

Britons prefer their cabbage white, Americans prefer it green. Over-ripe bananas are passed-up here and in most European countries, but people in many South American countries will not eat a banana unless it's brown.

Food manufacturers and processors know that color is just as important as flavor, quality, and price. Sometimes they give us colors more colorful than the real thing, as in jams, jellies, gelatines, and soft drinks. Our expectations of taste, based on color, are so strong that our eyes fool our tongues. In a recent test, subjects were given a lime-flavored drink that was orange in color. They described the taste as orange-flavored!

Market research tells us that our noses may lead us to the source of food, but our eyes make the choices. Only then do our taste buds take over. The colors that turn us on to foods most effectively are red, red-orange, orange, peach, yellow, light and dark green, brown, tan, and white.

White has always suggested purity and refinement, even in foods. However, with the swing to the organic and to whole foods, tans and browns are favored by many because they suggest earthiness and nutritional advantages.

The colors that turn people off in foods are grey, blue, black, vivid purple, and strong yellow-green. The latter shades are rarely found in natural foodstuffs, so the eye and the brain cannot associate those colors with anything appetizing. Many of those colors are not only unappetizing, but because of unpleasant associations, downright nauseating. Airlines avoid strong yellow-green in food and in interiors for obvious reasons!

Black is considered especially obnoxious because of its association to decay. Grey runs a close second; it seems old and flat in food. Vivid purple is found in flowers, but not in natural foodstuffs. Blue is moldy, but is passable in blue cheese because it is expected to be there. Blues are also acceptable in fruit-flavored foods such as ice-cream, yogurt, or drinks.

Frequently foods of close color families will contain the same vitamins and minerals, such as yellow foods for Vitamin A; red beets and tomatoes for iron and copper. Nutritionists often recommend getting many varieties of a color—a virtual rainbow—into your diet to be certain that you are getting all of your necessary nutrients. Food also takes healing qualities into the body, since it soaks up and stores the energies of light while it is growing.

Doctors have also found it necessary to eliminate some too-colorful food from the diet, especially those containing certain chemical additives. **Dr. Ben Feingold,** an allergist in San Francisco, has had great success in calming hyperactive children by deleting artificial flavoring, as well as artificial coloring from the diet.

Color and Diet

Not long ago, I was invited to a house-warming party. The hostess took several of us on a tour of the house and eventually ushered us into the brand new kitchen.

From ceiling to floor, including all of the appliances, as far as the eye could see, there was a brilliant orange. I contained myself as best I could, but as I looked around, I could see that everyone else was having the same problem. I was about to make my standard "I don't want to hurt her feelings but it's so ugly that I can't lie and say it's beautiful" comment, which is, "Well, it certainly is interesting." It covers a multitude of sins—from wonderfully interesting to hideously interesting. You get off the hook by leaving out the descriptive adjective.

Getting back to my hostess, she broke the ice by saying, "Awful, isn't it? I call it my obnoxious orange kitchen." It certainly was.

She told us that she is always dieting and thought that if she did the whole kitchen in orange, a color she detested, it would keep her out of the kitchen, and especially away from the refrigerator.

Her plan, however, was not working. She was gaining weight, rather than losing it. She asked me why, even though she hated the color and avoided the kitchen unless she had to prepare a meal, it wasn't working the way she had planned it.

I explained to her that orange is a prime appetite stimulant. Even though she was not spending a lot of time there, whenever she had to fix food for the family, she was surrounded by those huge doses of orange and her autonomic nervous system was working overtime. Red, orange, yellow, and brown have been shown to exert a measurable effect on the autonomic nervous system, which stimulates the appetite. She had been nibbling away while she cooked and most of the time was not even aware that she was eating.

Her approach was drastic, to say the least. You're much better off using a color from your preferred colortime in a room you have to spend so much time in. Being unhappy with your surroundings often leads to frustration. And we know where frustration leads us—right to the mouth.

Fast food restaurants are death to dieters, not only because of the french fries and milk shakes but because they discovered the secret of orange a long time ago. It's called "eat and run" orange. The appetite is stimulated and so are you—to eat fast and leave quickly and make room for the next victim.

In deference to the fast food industry, I have noticed a trend to creating "homier" atmospheres with wood trim and a little brick. But the major color is brown, which is essentially deepened orange. The message is there, but it has become much more subliminal.

Other subtle forms of orange are apricot, coral, and peach. These are truly delicious colors and some variation appears in every colortime. They are particularly pleasing tone for a dining room and make a warm and inviting background for guests. They have a less stimulating effect on appetite than orange does, and most people find them much easier on the eyes.

In the south of France near Cannes, where eating is an art, many restaurants are done in peachy tones. One particularly beautiful place called L'Oasis is done in deep greens and peach. Everything—china, linens, candles—is a medley of these two tones. From the moment you enter, you start to salivate. Guests are not obvious about their drooling, though—this is a very classy place.

Chocoholics

Chocolate brown, quiet as it is, is a prime culprit in the battle of the bulge. That universal favorite, that maker of cellulite, cavities, and midriff rolls—how could anything that tastes so good be so bad? I lean to carob, myself, but that is still the color of chocolate and carries the same associations.

In her book *The Joy Of Chocolate*, **Judith Olney** says of chocolate, "There is no greater symbol of self-indulgence...in the 16th century, chocolate was thought to be an aphrodisiac." (Maybe that explains the appeal.) Even today, chocolate is given as a gift of love.

Ms. Olney makes fabulous chocolate fantasies. I love her advice for anyone attempting to work with chocolate. She says, "Wear brown!" If you are a confirmed "chocoholic," you might feel very comfortable in a kitchen surrounded by rich woodtone cabinets and almond appliances. It would be like wallowing in a big hot fudge sundae. Chances are that you would not limit your kitchen colors to two, so you might accent your scheme with a non-food color such as blue. But avoid sweet suggestive shades, particularly maraschino cherry red!

Brown stimulates the appetite, especially when used with other sweet colors, such as peach or strawberry pink. The association is that of a dish of ice cream.

Blue dishes make an excellent background for food without stimulating the appetite. Violet, which is believed to be effective in depressing overactive glandular conditions, also depresses appetites. If you are trying to lose weight, the four colors to use cautiously in the kitchen would be red, orange, yellow, and brown.

Color may be wonderful food for thought, but if you are on a perpetual diet, avoid colors that give you thought for food.

Garnishing The Visual Appetite

If you have a finicky eater, young or old, deliberately use one of the colors mentioned above, or combinations of those colors, in place mats, table cloths, and other backgrounds for food. Change colors frequently to add an element of surprise. Try different colors and patterns in paper plates for an especially balky eater.

The food may have to be bland for those on limited diets, but the background doesn't have to be. A beautifully set table or a fun color combination can tempt the taste buds.

For The Sports Fans

At a Color Marketing Group meeting in San Francisco, I heard a fascinating talk given by **William Boyd** of **Beyl and Boyd,** a marketing and advertising firm. Mr. Boyd and his associates were retained by the owners of the **Vancouver Canucks** hockey team to help change the team's image in hopes of getting them out of a losing slump.

He demonstrated how he used the psychological impact of color and design to improve the performance of the Canadian players. Through extensive color research and many innovative design changes, the Canucks changed from sterile, cold, blue and white uniforms, which disappeared into the icy background, to a bold, menacing, brilliant yellow, red, and black. As Boyd put it, they were transformed from "Mighty Mice" to "Spider Men!"

Their performance improved, attendance rose, and everybody was happy—except the opposing teams. The Canucks went to the top of their division after the changes.

A midwest university football coach decided to use color to his advantage by painting the team's dressing room in dynamic red, and the room for the opposing team in little boy blue.

Both the **Philadelphia Phillies** baseball team and the **Philadelphia Eagles** pro-football team use "mood rooms" for relaxation. Color images are projected onto the walls and appropriate music is played in the background.

If a hue is brightened, muscular reaction and interest are heightened, so wearing a vivid leotard or pair of shorts to the gym is a good idea. If you are an owl and have to drag yourself out of bed in the morning to jog, struggle into a brilliant jogging suit.

Bright yellow tennis balls not only increase visibility but if you try harder to keep your eye on the ball because yellow is one of your favorite colors, you might stimulate yourself into winning. In research done at Wright State University, it was shown that children find it easier to catch balls in their favorite colors.

If you want to win at darts, use colored darts against a white background. Motor performance improves with that particular combination. The trick is to get your opponent to play on another dart board with the reverse combination!

Georgia State University psychologist **Morgan Worthy** concluded from studies that reactions are related to the color of your eyes. He feels that light-eyed people do better at deliberate tasks, and dark-eyed people have quicker reactions.

Translated into sports, this would mean that light-eyed people do better at self-paced sports, such as golf or archery, where they have more control. In football, light-eyed people tend to make better quarterbacks, according to Worthy.

Dark-eyed people, he feels, are best at instantaneous reactions, such as in tennis, hitting a baseball, or blocking in football.

He points out that watchdogs more often have dark eyes, but that stalkers such as pointers and setters have light eyes.

He is speaking in terms of general groups, so there is much room for exception (and for practice), but you might consider switching your sport to see what happens!

NBC sportscaster **Dick Enberg** likes to wear a red sportcoat when he delivers his play by play accounts of NFL football games and other sports events. He sees red as his good-luck color and it represents excitement to him, particularly the warm reds of his Sunset palette.

Red is such an "alive" color that it's natural for sports activities. Can you imagine a football jersey in seashell pink or mauve?

In the next chapter, you'll learn more of what colors say about you— and how to make them speak your language!

Chapter 7

Your Creative Energies and Color

Likes, Dislikes, and Secret Desires

In this chapter, you will find out more about your color preferences. There are individual colors within each colortime palette that you will like above all others. Every color is included in every colortime, in varying intensities and values. Each color evokes a different emotional response from you.

If you really dislike a color, it probably won't be in your preferred colortime, but you could be the exception to the rule.

That is why I treat each of my clients with an open mind, to try to find out about his or her orientation to color. However, since I can't be with you personally, there are certain universal thoughts and they should provide you with some useful observations about your personal color choices.

Refer to the page on which you wrote your favorite and least favorite colors. For your amazement and amusement, I have compiled what some of the experts, researchers and psychologists say about your color choices and added some of my own experiences with clients.

Please remember that your likes and dislikes can and do change over the years. Your responses will simply tell you where you are in your life right now. Your preferences may also indicate some of your secret desires. For example, red is considered the most ardent and passionate of all colors. You may not see yourself as ardent or passionate, but if red is your favorite color, maybe there are hidden traits just dying to be expressed (you little devil!).

Red

Like:

Just as red sits on top of the rainbow, you like to stay on top of things. You have a zest for life. Remember that red can speed up the pulse, increase the respiration rate, and raise blood pressure. It is associated with fire, heat, and blood, so it is impossible to ignore. And so are you (or would like to be).

The key words associated with red are winner, achiever, intense, impulsive, active, competitive, daring, aggressive. Red people are exciting, animated, optimistic, emotional, and extroverted. Desire is the key word (see "ardent" and "passionate" above), so they hunger for fullness of experience and living.

Now that you have all the good news, let's hear it for the bad news. Since you crave so much excitement in your life, routine can drive you bananas. Restlessness can make you fickle in your pursuit of new things to turn you on. It is hard for you to be objective and you can be opinionated. You have a tendency to listen to what others tell you and then do whatever you please. Patience is not one of your virtues.

However, you are an exciting person to be with, and always stimulating. The world would be a dull place without red people.

Dislike:

Since red is primarily associated with a zest for life, excitement, and passion, a dislike of this hue could mean that these feelings are a bit much for you to handle at this point in your life. Perhaps you are bothered by the aggressiveness and intensity that red signifies. Or perhaps you would really like more fulfillment but are afraid to get involved. People who are irritable, ill, exhausted, or bothered by many problems often reject red and turn to the calmer colors for rest and relaxation. They are very self-protective.

Pink

Like

This is a softened red, so it tempers passion with purity. It is associated with romance, sweetness, delicacy, refinement, and tenderness. Pink people are interested in the world around them, but they do not throw themselves into participating with the ardor of the red person. Violence in any form is upsetting to you.

At one time, pink was considered feminine, like the frosting on a little girl's birthday cake, but now it can be worn by men without embarrassment—after all, it is closely related to red.

If you love pink, you are talented and have subdued drive, charm, and warmth, and are probably an incurable romantic. Pink people are friendly but tend to keep inner feelings hidden.

The closer to orange pink gets, the warmer it is, and you are.

Dislike

Soft, medium tints do not evoke much emotion—many people (especially men) are indifferent to pink. It is sweetness, innocence, and naiveté—red with the passion removed. So if you dislike pink, you are looking for excitement in your life and pink simply will not do it for you.

Yellow

Like

Yellow is luminous and warm because it is strongly associated with sunshine. It sparkles with optimistic activity. Yellow people are highly original, imaginative, idealistic, creative, artistic, and often spiritual. You love novelty and challenge and have an inquiring mind. You are a reliable friend and confidant. Your ambitions are often realized, and you usually have a sunny disposition.

You are often egotistical, however, and do not like to be second best. You can be generous, but may be rather shy at heart and appear somewhat aloof as a result. You may be impatient with other people's ideas if they seem less well thought out than yours. You are genuinely concerned about the good of society, but generally spend more time talking about it than actually doing anything about it! Yellow people are perfectionists, but can also be joyful.

Dislike
If you dislike yellow, you usually dislike the qualities that this luminous color has. You are a realist—a practical, down-to-earth person and probably critical of others who are not. You are skeptical of new ideas and rather than try something innovative, you prefer to concentrate on things you know you can accomplish. Guaranteed results are important to you, because you like to protect yourself from disappointment.

Orange

Like
Orange is a combination of red and yellow, so it takes on many of the characteristics of both colors. It is vibrant and warm, like the autumn leaves. Orange has the physical force of red, but it is less intense, less passionate. Lovers of this color work and play hard, are adventurous and enthusiastic.

You are good-natured, expansive, and extroverted with a disposition as bright as your favorite color, and you like to be with people. Your ideas are unique and you have strong determination. You are more agreeable than aggressive.

Orange people can be fickle. It has been said that your latest friend is your best friend. Psychologist **Deborah Sharpe,** in an article by **Amy Gross** in *Mademoiselle* magazine, contends that a man whose favorite color is orange is the worst possible kind to marry. "He's great fun and a good mixer, but he's a love 'em, leave 'em kind." So as not to appear sexist, she also says this of women. She also says they are lousy housekeepers. Maybe you'd better check out his or her favorite color before you get involved!

Success in business can come easily to this gregarious, charming person. Since orange is a physical and mental stimulant, start the day by eating an orange while dressed in your orange terry bathrobe, to start your mind and body working together!

Dislike

Life is definitely not a dish of gumdrops for the rejecter of orange. Nothing flamboyant appeals to you. You dislike too much partying, hilarity, loud laughter, showing off, and obvious intimacy. As a result, you may be difficult to get to know, if not a loner. You prefer a few genuine close friends to a large circle of acquaintances and once you make a friend, they're your friend forever.

Brown

Like

The color of Mother Earth is the hue that is associated with substance and stability. A preference for brown means you have a steady, reliable character with a keen sense of duty and responsibility. You are the down-to-earth person with a subtle sense of humor. Browns love simplicity, comfort, quality, harmony, hearth, and home.

You are a loyal friend—understanding, but firm. Brown people have strong views and may be intolerant of others who think, talk, or act too quickly. You strive to be good money managers (we won't say "cheap") and drive a good bargain.

You are the person who might find it difficult to be carefree and spontaneous but will often rebel internally against accepting things the way they are. You feel very uncomfortable about losing control, but will work hard to change a situation that seems unjust or unfair.

You'd make a good marriage partner and a good parent because you have a strong need for security and a sense of belonging. Family life is very important to you.

Dislike

You probably fantasize about a lot of things, perhaps traveling with a circus or racing cars. Novelty excites you and routine drives you crazy. You are witty, impetuous, and generous. Living on a farm is not for you. Homespun people bore you. You do like people, but they must be bright and outgoing. A meaningful relationship with you could be risky business—it's hard to get you to sit still!

Beige

Like

Beige people have many of the same characteristics as brown, though they are probably less intense. Creamy beiges and honeyed tones take on a lot of yellow qualities, while rose beiges take on pink characteristics. You are warm, appreciate quality, and are carefully neutral in most situations. You are usually well-adjusted and practical.

Dislike

You are less frenetic and impetuous than a disliker of brown, but have many of the same characteristics. Beige represents to you a beige existence—boring and tiresome. You hate routine.

Green

Like

Nature's most plentiful color promises a balance between warmth and coolness, so green people are usually stable and balanced types. This is the good citizen, concerned parent, involved neighbor, and PTA member—the joiner of clubs and organizations. You are fastidious, kind, and generous.

It is important for you to win the admiration of peers so you are often a "do-gooder." You are a caring companion, loyal friend, partner or lover, with a high moral sense, and are super sensitive to doing the right thing.

You are intelligent and understand new concepts. You are less inclined, however, to risk something new than to do what is popular and conventional. The bad news about green people is that they often have big appetites for food. If you are dieting, it is difficult for you to lose your lumpies. The worst vice for a green is the tendency to gossip. Are you a little green with envy?

Dislike

Since lovers of green are usually very social, joiners, and "keep up with the Joneses" types, dislikers of green will often put those qualities down. You may have an unfulfilled need to be recognized that causes you to pull away from people rather than join them. You don't like thinking, looking, and doing things the way you see the majority of people thinking, looking, and doing them. Picnics, cocktail parties, and Saturday night at the Elks Club are not your thing.

Biliousness and certain body functions are often associated with yellow-green, as are snakes, lizards, dragons, and various other creepy-crawlies. Did something slithery frighten you as a child?

Blue

Like

The color of tranquility and peace, blue tends to be the most preferred color universally. Although cool and confident (or wishing to be), blues can be vulnerable. You are trusting and need to be trusted. You are sensitive to the needs of others and form strong attachments, and are deeply hurt if your trust has been betrayed.

Blue people aspire to harmony, serenity, patience, perseverance, and peace. You are somewhat social but prefer sticking to your own close circle of friends. You think twice before speaking or acting out. You are generally conservative, even-tempered, and reliable.

Because of the highly developed sense of responsibility of the blue personality, you must be careful of perfectionist tendencies that may make you unrealistically demanding. Your gentleness, however, will win out.

If you have trouble falling asleep at night, think of the blues in your colortime, or count blue sheep.

Dislike

A dislike of blue may mean restlessness—a need to break away from the sameness that bores you. Perhaps you would like to change your job, or even your life, and long for more excitement. You might be tired of being "depended on," but your conscience makes you stay. You wish that you were either wealthy or brilliant (or both) because that would enable you to have all the good things in life without working so hard. Deeper blues may mean sadness and melancholy to you—blue may simply give you the blues.

Blue-green

Like

Since this is a marriage of the colors previously mentioned, many of the traits will be combined, but there are added dimensions. You are neat (to the point of fussiness) and well-groomed. You are sensitive, but also sophisticated, self-assured, and (usually) stable.

You help others and usually manage your own affairs very well. Courtesy and charm are characteristics, too. But narcissism is a key word here. Green-blues love to dress up to get the admiration of others, but along with admiration, you may also provoke some of the "blue-green-eyed monsters."

Dislike

Since love of blue-green means orderliness and neatness, dislike of blue-green means that, as messy as you'd like to be, a little voice inside you (was it your mother or your father?) keeps telling you to clean up your room. As much as you try to ignore it, it won't go away. You would really love to relax more and not pay attention to petty details. You really prefer earthy types to fussy people.

Purple

Like

This hue has an aura of mystery and intrigue. The purple person is enigmatic and highly creative, with a quick perception of spiritual ideas. Purple is often preferred by artists. People who like to consider themselves different from the common herd or unconventional often prefer purple.

You are often generous and, at times, charming. Purple is also associated with wit, keen observation, super sensitivity, vanity, and moodiness. Because purple is a combination of red and blue, which are opposites in many ways, you often have conflicting traits. You are constantly trying to balance those opposites—the excitement of red with the tranquility of blue. It has been said that purple people are easy to live with but hard to know. You can be secretive, so that even when you seem to confide freely, your closest friends never completely understand you.

Dislike

If you are anti-purple, you need sincerity, honesty, and a lack of pretense in your life. You do not like to get involved unless you know exactly what you are getting yourself into. You usually exercise good judgment. Frankness is a quality you look for in your friends. You may not have a particular artistic talent, but you would make a good critic!

Because of purple's association with royalty, purple may seem puffed up and pompous to you, or because of its association with mourning, you may see it as melancholy. In certain areas of the world, bright purple is worn by ladies of questionable reputation. Perhaps you are still hearing that little voice in your ear telling you that nice people don't wear purple.

Lavender

Like

People who love this tint use it sometimes to the exclusion of all other colors. Just as with purple, this person likes to be considered different. You are quickwitted, though usually not intellectual.

The lavender person seeks refinement in life. Yours is a fantasy land where ugliness and the baser aspects of life are ignored. Outward appearances are very important. Gentility and sentimental leanings also go along with this color, as do romance, nostalgia, and delicacy. Since lavender is first cousin to purple, you may aspire to creativity, but if not capable of it, you tend to encourage those who do have talent.

Dislike

Yours is a no-nonsense approach to life. You don't like others to be coy with you—you would rather they be direct. Nostalgia is not your thing; you live in the present. Just as with the anti-purple people, you don't like superficiality in manners or appearance and you usually let people know about it (or wish that you had). You may also see lavender as insipid or aging.

Grey

Like

People who prefer this most neutral of all shades are carefully neutral about life. You like to protect yourself from the hectic world, wrapping yourself with the security blanket of a noncommittal color. You prefer a secure, safe, balanced existence, and so, unlike the reds in life, you never crave real excitement, just contentment. It is important for you to maintain the status quo.

You have often made compromises in your lifestyle. You are practical and calm and do not like to attract attention. You are willing to work hard (the grey flannel suit) and to be of service. You are the middle-of-the-road type, cool, conservative, composed, and reliable.

If this makes you feel like a little grey mouse, the consolation is that you will often use a splash of color to make some sort of statement. So you really aren't all that dull!

Dislike
To dislike grey is to dislike neutrality. You would rather be right or wrong, but never indifferent. Routine bores you. You look for a richer, fuller life. This may lead you to get into one involvement, hobby, or interest after another in the pursuit of happiness. Grey may mean eerie ghosts, ashes, cobwebs, and the dust of a haunted house, or other scary grey things.

Taupe

Like
This color also speaks of neutrality, but combines the character and dependability of grey with the warmth of beige. You like classic looks and are careful about allowing too much excitement into your life. You're practical, fair, well-balanced, and would make a good arbitrator.

Dislike
If taupe doesn't appeal to you, it may be because it is so balanced and classic. You'd rather make a more definite statement, whether with color or otherwise. You're probably not known for your subtlety.

Black

Like
This is rarely chosen as a favorite color because it is actually the negation of color. The person who chooses black may have a number of

conflicting attitudes. You may be conventional, conservative, and serious, or you may like to think of yourself as rather worldly or sophisticated, a cut above everyone else, or very dignified.

You may also want to have an air of mystery, or, as in the language of the proverbial black negligee, be very sexy. Wit, cleverness, personal security, and prestige are very important to you.

Dislike
Since black is the negation of color, it may be a total negative to you. It is the eternal mystery, the bottomless pit, the black hole, the halloween witch and her black cat. It may represent death and mourning to you. Things that go bump in the night are black. Were you frightened by the dark in your childhood? That experience could be buried in the darkest recesses of your mind and may still haunt you when you look at anything black. Black may simply be too heavy or depressing for you to handle at this point in your life.

You are uncomfortable with the super-sophisticated and feel insecure in their company. You like real people and are not dazzled by dignitaries.

White

Like
White is cleanliness and purity, and those who prefer white are neat and immaculate in their clothing and homes. You are inclined to be a cautious buyer and shrewd trader, but critical and fussy. If you got a spot on your tie or scarf in a restaurant, you would summon a glass of water immediately to clean it off. White also signifies a self-sufficient person and, occasionally, innocence. It is a recall of youth and simplicity.

Dislike
Since white represents cleanliness and purity, to dislike white does not exactly mean that you are a messy person, but it does mean that you have never been obsessed with order. You are not very fussy. Things that are a little off-center are much more interesting to you than those that are perfectly in line. A little dust on the shelves or on yourself doesn't throw you into a spasm of cleaning. You are not very uptight and are easy to be with. You may see white as sterile and connect it with nurses' uniforms, doctors, and worst of all (for many people), dentists.

Changing Colors and Changing Lives

If your favorite (or least favorite) is actually a combination color—such as golden rust, which is a combination of brown and orange—you have some of the traits of both hues and a more complex personality. Some of these characteristics may actually seem in conflict with each other. For example: Brown is emphasis on family life, whereas orange can be fickle. How much of you is orange and how much is brown?

The closer to its neighbor a color gets, the more it will take on the personality of that color. A red-purple is more exciting than a blue-purple. A yellow-orange is happier than a yellow-green.

Lightening a hue takes some of the strength out of it. For example: If your favorite is a cream color, this is the lightest combination of yellow and brown. It will never sparkle the way yellow does because it has been paled, yet the effect can still be cheering and warm. The more yellow you add, the happier it is and you are.

Darkening a hue adds dignity, depth, and strength. Shades like wine, evergreen, deep purple, navy blue, and charcoal grey take the basic characteristics of those hues and make them more conservative, refined, and restrained. For example: Deep wine red is positive and assured, but certainly more dignified than cherry red.

Watch TV commercials to see how color is used on spokespeople. A man in a dark jacket and subtle tie convinces you to buy various kinds of aspirin or to put your money in his hands. His attire gives him more credibility than he would have in a neon-bright sweater.

Faber Birren, author of many books on color, tells us that to like a basic color or colors is to be essentially simple and open in character, to have strong and well-directed interests. To prefer an "off color" such as blue-green rather than blue or green, or dark wine instead of primary red, indicates that natural preferences have been tempered over the years. This person has done something to alter his or her character.

Birren believes that to like refined or gentle colors is to show a wish for peace and security, for freedom from care or worries. He also believes that nearly all people have made changes in their favorite color choices over the years.

Many people who have remade their lives choose new colors to go with their new selves. Some of my clients who are in periods of change, often after a divorce, will say to me, "I wish I could throw everything away and start all over again!"

Shadow or Sunlight? Lifting Your Spirits

Faber Birren tells us: "If light colors are preferred, this person longs for an escape from the harsher aspects of life. If deep colors are preferred, this person may resent the world and be inclined toward aggressiveness."

Dr. Jean Rosenbaum, a psychiatrist, has written about color and lifestyle in a book called *Is Your Volkswagon A Sex Symbol?* He believes that color has always had special symbolic meaning with regard to clothes, and psychological meaning in that since color reflects personality and mood. He says that traditional ideas about color may have passed into folklore, but the psychology behind these ideas is still valid, such as black for mourning, white for purity, etc.

He feels that dark colors continue to mean depression and bright colors to signify happiness. We have to be careful not to generalize and believe that every time you wear dark clothing you are depressed. But if you wear dark shades habitually, to the exclusion of most other colors, you may be hiding an emotional problem. A heavy mood may make you unconsciously choose heavy colors.

Dr. Rosenbaum speculates that if you are anxious and depressed, you might prefer shadow to sunlight. In an effort to avoid people, you might be unconsciously choosing negative colors. He says: "It is possible to use color to get over a particular mood or to convey a desired impression. The next time you feel sad or depressed . . . if you have dark or neutral colors on, change to a brighter color. You may be amazed at what it does for your spirits."

He suggests that you wear bright, positive clothes on days on which you have to make a special presentation. He feels that they might help you to convey that you have something constructive to offer.

Some experts feel that bright colors signify a brighter mood—they are equated with an optimistic, outgoing, and creative personality. This may be true to some extent, but people who wear bright colors in preference to all others may have a real need to attract attention. As in every other area of life, the key word is balance. Your moods change in intensity and so should your colors.

Interestingly, if you prefer neutrals to all other colors, you tend to be more secure than those people who constantly use bright colors. Dr. Rosenbaum contends that people who like neutrals are kind, firm, and logical, and prefer discipline to disorder. You'd make a good teacher.

Dr. Deborah Sharpe, in the article by **Amy Gross,** states that people who prefer drab and neutral colors tend to be more secure than those who like bright colors, but before you start to feel too smug, she feels that you are also repressed and less emotional.

She feels the response to color is a primitive one, emotional rather than intellectual for most people. How people respond to color offers some insight into their degree of emotional control, their social orientation, their maturity, and their creativity.

She does not believe that having a favorite color means that you surround yourself with it or wear it constantly. It just means that "whenever that color is viewed, something special happens. You are turned on by it . . . the only way to change your favorite color is to change your personality."

She believes that the number of favorites a person has tells you something about him or her and maintains that a "good solid person has one favorite and likes one or two others. If someone says I love all colors, her personality has not crystallized yet. She has no structure. She's flighty." If she chooses one color to the exclusion of all others . . . "she's too rigid and she's overstructured." (I am assuming that Dr. Sharpe would also include men in her suppositions!)

In some cases, fragmented colors can indicate a fragmented personality when used to an extreme. Wearing inappropriate clothes or fiercely clashing combinations can show an emotional problem or mental illness. Total disharmony on the outside can mean inner turmoil.

When I lived in Washington, D.C., I would often see a woman in her 50's window shopping and walking in and out of all the stores. She always wore outfits of only one color, but every variation of that color imaginable. If it was her green day, she would wear every possible green—all of them clashing.

She was utterly oblivious to the stares of other shoppers and salespeople. She was off in a world of her own, and her color combinations were an instant clue to her mental state.

In analyzing color, when we try to determine why people choose what they choose, we have to be careful not to overgeneralize. Some people select—and many times out of necessity—dark shades because they don't show the dirt or they choose neutrals because they go with everything. But they are still giving us a message about themselves, and the message is, "I'm practical."

My own experience with clients has been that many artistic types will say they love all colors and absolutely refuse to commit to a particular color or colors. However, I don't see that as a fragmented personality because they are accustomed to working with all colors.

Robert Sherman, who, with his brother, **Richard,** composed the music for many Disney movies, including "Mary Poppins" (remember "Supercalifragilisticexpialidocious?") and has composed for Broadway musicals, is also an artist. He says that when he is not writing songs, he is painting pictures, and has found over the years that the one activity helps him get away from the other so that he can return to each refreshed.

Bob and his wife Joyce each have a wonderful sense of color and have used all of the colortime palettes to evoke various moods in their beautiful Beverly Hills home.

Seeing Music in Color

I have often wondered if composers "see" music in color. I asked **John Williams,** who has written musical scores for such films as "Star Wars," and "E.T.," and is the conductor of the **Boston Pops,** if he had ever written music to correspond to color in a film. He said that when he composed the score for "Close Encounters," he developed a distinctive musical signature to announce the presence of something mysterious in outer space. The sound of each note was given a different color on the screen.

John told me about a musical work by Russian composer **Alexandre Scriabin** that was performed at Carnegie Hall in New York in 1915. It must have been one of the first "light shows." The audience sat in total darkness while the music was played and colored lights chosen by the composer were shown against a backdrop.

Critics panned the show as too "disturbing." Can you imagine the reaction of those same critics to today's riotously lighted rock concerts with their rainbows of colored laser lights?

Because my husband was very involved in the production of the first "Star Wars" concert, which was conducted by **Zubin Mehta** at the Hollywood Bowl and accompanied by a laser light show, I was able to follow the project from its inception. The combination of music and light was pure magic and the audience reaction was deafening!

The Rainbow Book, a collection of essays and illustrations devoted to rainbows, tells about famed artist **Wassily Kandinsky,** who compared the sounds of musical instruments to colors. He perceived light, warm red and medium yellow as strong, vigorous, and triumphant—the sounds of trumpets. Light, cool red hues were violins.

Vermilion (orange-red) was a drum to Kandinsky, and orange a church bell. Yellow he "heard" as a bugle, green as the middle notes of a violin, and light blue as a flute. The notes of a cello were darker blue. Black or deepest blue were organ tones, and violet made the sound of an English Horn or one of the woodwinds.

The classic film "Fantasia" showed how effective the marriage of music, film, and color can be. No one who has seen "The Wizard of Oz" can forget Dorothy's dramatic journey from the black and white scenery of Kansas over the rainbow to the brilliantly colored land of Oz, or her enchanting dance down the yellow brick road to the Emerald City.

The recent film version of the musical, "The Wiz," contained entire scenes that were shot alternately in hot and cool colors to change the mood of the scene. **Quincy Jones** told me how challenging and exciting it was for him to change the mood of the music so that it worked to express the shifting colors.

Alive
With Color

Many composers, like **Sammy Cahn, Arthur Schwartz, Charles Fox,** and **John Green,** see connecting links between music and color. Jazz is referred to as either "hot" or "cool." Without descriptive, colorful lyrics, there would be no "blue moons," "purple mountain majesties," or "yellow ribbons" to tie around the old oak tree. Even Kermit the frog couldn't tell us "It's Not Easy Being Green." As the great **Pablo Casals** once said, "All music is a rainbow."

Arthur Hamilton, Vice President of the Academy of Motion Picture Arts and Sciences, wrote one of the bluest of the blues songs, "Cry Me A River." Arthur told me that he sent a bouquet of brilliant flowers (in the AM colortime) to **Peggy Lee** when she was opening in a new act, signing his card with the words "Sing a rainbow." Peggy called him and said, "That's a great song title—if you don't use it, I will!" He did, and the new tune was used in a film appropriately titled, "Pete Kelly's Blues."

Some artists prefer to work within a particular colortime almost exclusively. When I met the late **Princess Grace** of Monaco, she had just been featured in a magazine article showing her floral collages. Her work was most often done in the Sunrise palette, and sometimes in Sunlight shades, but rarely in the Sunset colortime.

She told me that she chose Sunrise colors for drama in clothing and makeup, such as for photographs for a magazine cover, but that she preferred Sunlight colors for her ordinary "everyday" life. She never wore the Sunset colors, she said, because they simply weren't "her." When I asked her what her very favorite color was, she replied with a princessly smile, "Regal purple, of course."

Pastel Mothers and Dark Fathers

Our daughter, **Lori,** is an art therapist and photographer. Her experiences, which are borne out by the writings of experts like Faber Birren, tell us that art therapy has done a great deal to help mental patients "open up." Children, for instance, may have difficulty articulating their thoughts, yet express themselves easily with crayons and paints. It is a normal tendency for children to use bright colors, with the luminous warm shades often the most preferred. When a child uses black crayons frequently, it is an indication of pent-up emotions, a too-rigid upbringing, or a very restricted environment.

Love of red is quite common in children and shows a carefree spirit. Immature behavior and over-dependency on adults go with a love of yellow. A preference for green shows a well-adjusted, balanced personality, just as it does with adults. Mothers are often painted in pastel shades, and darker colors tend to be used for disciplinarian daddies. Brothers and sisters are painted in colors appropriate to the way the child perceives them.

Children are essentially quite primitive in their color choices, which may remain the same through adolescence. Adulthood tends to bring a refining of color preferences.

Touches of bright color are used in children's wards in hospitals to downplay the institutional look. Nurses are often encouraged to wear colorful smocks. Warm tones in hospital settings should be cheerful and not too intense; yellows and yellow-greens should be used cautiously as they can cast a sickly pallor on the faces of the young patients.

Studies have shown that color can actively aid mental growth and performance. A German psychologist found that children tested in rooms with beautiful soft yellow, orange, or light blue walls showed IQ scores 12 points higher than average. When similar groups of children were tested in rooms of white, black, or brown, their scores were 14 points below average. In addition, children who played in beautifully coordinated rooms with bright toys developed positive, friendly, social behavior.

From "Ho-Hum" to "Wow"

How many times have you heard someone, perhaps yourself, say, I can't wear that color, I'm too big (or too heavy)? **Marti P.** had seen me on TV and came to me to have her colors done. I suggested a vibrant blue-green teal to go with her outgoing, bubbly personality. She said that she never wore bright colors because she was too "big-boned" and tall.

I convinced her that the two things about yourself that you cannot change are your height and your bones, so why condemn yourself to a lifetime of the dreary drabs?

Soon after that, she was mistress of ceremonies for a program that I participated in. She wore that gorgeous blue-green on the stage and must have gotten a hundred compliments that day. She is a vivacious Sunset personality and would sparkle in a potato sack, but the color of that dress and all of those wonderful comments made her feel sensational. Her self-image needed that. She (and you) should never settle for "ho-hum" when you can have "wow!"

Bright colors were often considered "vulgar" or "cheap" until about 1960. Pastels and muted colors were thought to be more elegant. There are many today who feel the same way and stay with neutral, drab, and dark colors because in their social circles, those shades are associated with status—not unlike wearing school colors.

Some people continue to think of bright colors as tacky or ostentatious, but their numbers seem to be dwindling. Researchers tell us that lower socioeconomic groups often choose bright colors to compensate for bleak surroundings. Since the color explosion of the 1960's, the lines separating classes of society have become blurred. People often use pure, rich colors to stimulate lives that might be dull or monotonous. Even in parts of the world where there seems to be a total lack of color in the terrain, there is always color to be found. This has been obvious to me in so many areas where I have traveled.

In Morocco, for instance, the countryside and the small homes are sand-colored. The women wear dark caftans and veils. They appear small, dark, and somber. One day I saw a group of women taking off their outer garments so that they could do their weekly wash in a stream. I was amazed and delighted to see the most vivid combinations of designs and colors imaginable in the garments they wore under the caftans.

Conclusion

Unless you live in a cave or a nudist camp, you have to wear clothes. Every day of your life you send messages out via your colors. Why not choose your very best colors for those messages, whether you're wearing a business suit or a jogging suit? You're painting a picture for your own enjoyment that can't help but spill over to those around you.

Use your colortime palettes as an expression of you, to help you feel more rested, energized, creative, and confident, and to make your home a true source of comfort. You deserve it.

I hope this book has given you useful and enjoyable information. Your life may never be the same—you may find yourself studying the celebrities on TV or the person in front of you at the check-out stand, and driving your friends, family, and salespeople crazy with your new-found knowledge. (Careful—lighting and makeup can be deceptive, so what you are seeing on the TV screen may be *reel* coloring instead of *real* coloring!) You're apt to look at the colors they choose—for their clothes, their kitchens, and their cars—with new insights. It can be great fun and a wonderful way to heighten your awareness of the world around you.

Use your colortime palettes as an expression of the real you—from the colortime that makes you look and feel your absolute best, to the colortime ambiance you create in your surroundings. Make every day a special day...come alive—with color!

Bibliography

Architectural Digest, "Architectural Digest Visits Andy Williams." December 1978.

Birren, Faber. *Color, a Survey in Words and Pictures*. New Hyde Park, New York: University Books, 1963.

---. *Color in Your World*. New York: Macmillan Publishing Co., Inc., 1962.

---. *Color Psychology and Color Therapy*. Secaucus, N.J.: Citadel Press, 1980.

Bornstein, Marc and Marks, Lawrence. "Color Revisionism." *Psychology Today*, January 1982.

Clark, Linda. *The Ancient Art of Color Therapy*. Old Greenwich, Connecticut: Devin-Adair Co., 1975.

Goldstein, Kurt. *The Organism*. Lexington, Massachusetts: D.C. Heath & Co., 1939.

Graham, F. Lanier. *The Rainbow Book*. New York: Vintage Books, 1979.

Gross, Amy. "How to Read a Person Like a Coloring Book." *Mademoiselle Magazine*, March 1976.

Hellman, Hal. "Guiding Light." *Psychology Today*. April 1982.

The International Journal for Biosocial Research. "The Effects of Color Psycho-Dynamics, Environmental Modification Upon Psycho-Physiological and Behavioral Reactions of Severely Handicapped Children." Vol. 3, 1982.

Kavner, Richard and Dusky, Lorraine. *Total Vision*. New York: A & W Publishers, 1978.

Luce, Gay Gaer. *Body Time*. New York: Random House, 1969.

Luce, Gay Gaer and Segal, Julius. *Insomnia*. Garden City, New York: Doubleday, 1969.

Luscher, Max. *Luscher Color Test*. New York: Random House, 1969.

Molloy, John and Humber, Thomas. *Dress for Success*. New York: Warner Books, 1975.

Olney, Judith. *The Joy of Chocolate*. Woodbury, New York: Barron's Educational Series, 1982.

Ott, John. *Health and Light*. Old Greenwich, Connecticut: Devin-Adair Co., 1973.

Rosenbaum, Jean. *Is Your Volkswagen a Sex Symbol?* New York: Hawthorn Books, 1972.

Schauss, Alexander. "The Application of Behavioral Photo Biology to Human Aggression: Baker-Miller Pink." *The International Journal for Biosocial Research*. Vol. 2, 1981.

Sharpe, Deborah T. *The Psychology of Color and Design*. Chicago: Nelson-Hall Co., 1974.

Von Furstenburg, Egon with Duhe, Camille. *The Power Look.* New York: Holt, Rinehart, and Winston, 1978.

Worthy, Morgan. *Eye Color, Sex, and Race—Keys to Human and Animal Behavior* Anderson, South Carolina: Droke House/Hallux, 1974.

Zunin, Leonard with Zunin, Natalie. *Contact, The First Four Minutes.* New York: Ballantine Books, 1973.

Index

Alive
With Color